MISSION:
POSSIBLE

MISSION: POSSIBLE

The Challenge of Mission Today

By
Gottfried Oosterwal

Southern Publishing Association, Nashville, Tennessee

Copyright © 1972 by
Southern Publishing Association
2nd Printing 1975
Library of Congress
Catalog Card No. 72-95276
SBN 8127-0066-X

This book was
Edited by Richard Coffen
Designed by Dean Tucker
Cover photo by James Turner

Text set 10/11 Melior
Printed on Clear Spring Offset
Cover stock: Scott Mobile C1S

Printed in U.S.A.

Dedication

In gratitude and admiration, dedicated to a great missionary, *Elder Klaas Tilstra,* whose life, work, and faith showed me the answer to the challenge of mission today.

Acknowledgments

I wish to express my gratitude to the editors of *Insight* and *Spectrum* for permission to print material presented in this book on the challenge of mission today, which originally appeared in those publications.

A special word of thanks I offer to Margaret McFarland, who stimulated, encouraged, and equipped me to have MISSION: POSSIBLE published. And after all that, she did the real busy work on this volume.

All Biblical references are from the New English Bible.[1] Quotations from the writings of Ellen G. White are taken from the standard editions of her works and have been footnoted at the end of each chapter.

---

[1] The New English Bible. Copyright, The Delegates of the Oxford University Press and The Syndics of the Cambridge University Press, 1961, 1970. Reprinted by permission.

Contents

Introduction 11

Mission 1. The Challenge of Mission Today 15

Mission 2. Continuity and Change in Adventist Mission 23

Mission 3. Seventh-day Adventist Mission in the Seventies.... 43

Mission 4. Christ's Mission and Ours 69

Mission 5. That Curious Word *Missionary* 83

Mission 6. The World Our Destination 93

Mission 7. The Role of the Laity 103

Bibliography 121

Introduction

Mission: Possible presents a selection of articles and studies, now revised and edited, focusing on the challenge of mission today. It is a challenge of vaster scope than we realize, unfortunately.

Chapter 1 introduces the challenge of mission today by underlining the necessity that mission must rest upon every Christian. It then moves into the need for a flexible mission endeavor and closes with the challenge to seek the solutions that will make Seventh-day Adventist mission possible.

Chapter 2, first published as a contribution to a book honoring Dr. Edward Heppenstall,[1] who for many years has stimulated Adventists in their ministry for Christ, traces my analysis of the development of the Seventh-day Adventist concept of mission. It presents the challenge posed by the recent Adventist discovery of *the whole world* as the object of its mission, that is, the over two billion non-Christians besides the mushrooming number of secularists and nominal Christians who lack a deep personal relationship with Jesus Christ.

The third chapter, "Seventh-day Adventist Mission in the Seventies," analyzes the missionary situation of the Adventist Church today and discusses the implications for the strategy, the forms, and the priorities of its mission. This chapter, originally prepared as a lecture for the Mission Emphasis Week at Andrews University in February, 1970, appeared in the spring issue of the journal *Spectrum* that same year.[2]

Our answers to the many challenges of mission today, such as the new forms and strategies which our missionary endeavors may need or our decisions regarding policies and priorities, all depend on our concept of mission. Obviously, then, we need a clear, Biblical theology of mission. What is mission? What are its goals and objectives? How does the mission of the church relate to Christ's mission? Chapter 4, "Christ's Mission and Ours," seeks to challenge the present generation of Christians to rediscover that Biblical concept of mission, without which a missionary movement flounders like a ship without a compass. This chapter was prepared for a discussion group of Protestant and Roman Catholic theologians in order to briefly present the Adventist concept of mission. Through its insight into Christ's ministry in the heavenly sanctuary, the Adventist Church can substantially contribute to a Christian understanding of mission.

The terms "mission" and "missionary" have a confusing plurality of meanings in our day, inside as well as outside the church. They range from "Apollo mission" to "foreign mission" to "search-and-destroy mission." In many areas of the world the terms "mission" and "missionary" can no longer be used because of certain historical connections with imperialism and colonialism. Should we drop the terms, as some suggest, and substitute "expatriate," "fraternal worker," or "apostle" for them? The answer to the question hinges largely on what the Bible means by a missionary. This challenge, presented in chapter 5, was given as a lecture for the Mission Emphasis Week at Southern Missionary College in the spring of 1971.

Success or failure in mission is closely related to the believers' concepts of and attitudes toward the *world* as the object of their mission. Ancient Israel failed because it shut itself away from the world. Many Christians today fail because they have become so absorbed by the world that they have lost their sense of mission. Yet, an involvement in the world and its activities, as salt and yeast, as well as a certain separateness—both are necessary for the church to accomplish its mission. Chapter 6, first published in the December

15, 1970, issue of *Insight*,[3] explores these challenges.

When our Lord sent His disciples as His witnesses into all the world, He thereby commissioned *the whole church*. By virtue of their baptism, then, all members of the church participate alike, in essence, in the apostolic succession (authority), in the priesthood (ministry), in the worship, in the spiritual gifts, and in the mission of the church. The rediscovery of the missionary role of the laity as the "people claimed by God for his own, to proclaim the triumphs of him who has called you" (1 Peter 2:9) is the true answer to the challenge of mission today. Only when the church as a whole is totally involved—and not just a professional leadership and clergy—will it accomplish its purpose.

The final chapter, "The Role of the Laity," contends that this rediscovery of the Biblical role of the laity is essential not only to the revival and reformation the church today seeks but also to the finishing of God's mission on earth. This study on the Biblical role of the laity appears in print for the first time here, giving in a nutshell what a forthcoming book on laymen and other ministers will present in greater detail.

Most chapters were written specifically for Seventh-day Adventists. However, fellow Christians may discover in these pages how much Adventists have in common with them, how much Adventist mission can contribute to the advance of the gospel in all the world, and how much Adventists must yet learn. No matter who dedicates himself to spreading the gospel, he will find that there are basic principles that he will need to recognize and follow. Adventist and non-Adventist alike will need to find out what they are and how to put them into operation.

Teachers and students may find in these chapters useful material for classes and stimulation for further research. Local congregations may find them profitable for group discussion, prayer meetings, and as background material for mission reports. Ministers and church leaders, hopefully, will find some stimulating ideas for sermon preparation on mission, for guiding the church in its missionary outreach, for the setting of priorities, and for the developing of plans to hasten the finishing of God's work.

May God use this volume to stimulate our thinking on mission and our rededication to Him who has called us into His marvelous light and to arouse us to action so that the whole world may soon know of Jesus Christ, our Saviour and Lord. His mission brought us into the kingdom of God. With that great love before us, we really have no other choice but to become ambassadors of reconciliation ourselves, do we? (2 Corinthians 5: 14-20.)

GOTTFRIED OOSTERWAL
Andrews University
Berrien Springs, Michigan

[1] *The Stature of Christ:* Festschrift honoring Elder E. Heppenstall. Loma Linda, California, 1970, pp. 45-57.
[2] "SDA Mission in the 70's," *Spectrum,* Spring, 1970, pp. 5-20.
[3] "The World, My Destination," *Insight,* December 15, 1970, pp. 11-16.

The Challenge of Mission Today

Mission is the heartbeat of the church. If it stops, the church ceases to be. Each institution, every program, and any activity of the church has meaning—and a right to exist—only if it participates in mission. And every believer by baptism not only publicly declares himself a follower of Jesus Christ but also pledges himself to work with Him for the salvation of men.[1] Mission, then, is the hallmark of a Christian, his test of faith. No believer, really, can sing in church, "Redeemed, redeemed, Redeemed by the blood of the Lamb," or pray, "Thy kingdom come," without thereby binding himself to participate in Christ's own mission. Nobody can truly say that he belongs to God's own people unless he serves Christ as a missionary.[2]

Each generation of believers, however, must reassess the task of presenting Christ to the world so that it can fulfill its mission in its own particular way. Why?

Personal Commitment

First, because mission involves personal commitment. It is accomplished only through individual men and women in whom Christ lives and works. Mission is our spiritual heritage. But like the men in Jesus' parable who received talents from their boss, each individual believer has to accept Christ's spiritual legacy and work with it in order to possess it according to his own personality and ability. (Matthew 25:14-30.)

The Christian who receives the legacy of mission and thinks that it will work of its own accord is mistaken. He is like the man who buried his talent in the ground. Mission does not work that way. It succeeds only through personal acceptance, personal effort, and personal commitment.

A New World

Second, because each generation of believers faces a different world. This seems to be more true of our present generation than of any other in history. Today we face such challenges as the population, transportation, communication, and knowledge explosions; the resurgent world religions and the rise of thousands of new religions from Japan to Jamaica, from California to New Caledonia; urbanization, secularization, and nationalism; the tremendous social, economic, and political gaps between East and West; and the ongoing revolutionary changes in all cultures. To the people born in the twenties and earlier our present world looks like a city just struck by a terrible earthquake, immediately followed by a tornado. Roads are blocked, institutions have collapsed, and gone are the familiar landmarks by which people once oriented themselves.

Confusion reigns about what to do first and how to spend the limited funds. But since the object of our mission is the world, the world for which Christ died (John 3:16-18), the world into which He has sent us (John 17: 18), each generation must come to grips with that different world in which it lives. This may be the greatest challenge of mission today.

Present Truth

Third, because, as the history of both God's revelation and mission evidences, each generation has a particular message to proclaim and its own task to fulfill in the world. Many years ago Seventh-day Adventists adopted the term "present truth" to describe its commission—truth relevant to a particular time in a very special, historical situation. Present truths may never have been taught before, or they may be old truths reiterated with a new emphasis. The challenge of mission today is to find God's very special truth for our time and our world and then to accept it ourselves and proclaim it to others.

A New Revival

Fourth, because the Christian churches and the whole position of Christianity in the world have changed. On the one hand, we have seen a liberal theology robbing the Christian message of its urgency and clarity, a reinterpretation of mission in terms of social and economic action, and a form of ecumenism which bears in it the danger of making the churches disobedient to God and to His Word. On the other hand, revolutionary changes have marked the Roman Catholic Church as it has rediscovered the Biblical doctrines of righteousness by faith, the missionary nature of the church, the authority of Scripture, and the evangelical *aggiornamento* of Vatican II. Moreover, a Biblical and spiritual revival has revitalized the evangelical churches by emphasizing Christ's soon coming, the need for conversion and Christian perfection, and an unprecedented worldwide evangelism that is leading millions of people from all races, nations, and cultures to Christ. Currently over three fourths of all American missionaries come from churches outside the framework of the National Council of Churches.

These challenges to our own spirituality and concept of mission deserve our attention even more, because the number of people in today's world who have never heard about Christ is eight to ten times greater than in the days of the Apostle Paul. Barely 20 percent of the world population today is Christian, and a decade from now it may be only 15 percent. And though the Lord has never told us that the whole world will accept Him, He did definitely commission us to proclaim the gospel to every person on earth. Since Christ died for all of them, they all have a right to know it. Therein lies the challenge of our generation.

A Changing Church

Fifth, because the Seventh-day Adventist Church changes with each generation. From a small band of believers in North America and Europe, it has grown into the most widespread single Protestant missionary organization, with nearly two and a half million members. From a largely Western church, it suddenly has become a largely non-white and non-Western church, with some 80 percent of its membership living outside North America. Because the rapid and tremendous growth of the Adventist Church is largely confined to Latin America, Africa, and Asia, our church membership in North America will barely reach 10 percent by the end of this decade. Furthermore, with 65 to 70 percent of the population in the Third World under twenty-five, the Adventist Church also consists largely of young people.

This trend presents a number of very special challenges to the Adventist Church today, challenges ranging from proportionate representation in the highest executive bodies for these new churches and the priorities of how and where to spend the "Adventist dollar" to the training of an African, Asian, and Latin American corps of missionaries and church leaders and a structural reorganization reflecting the new missionary situation in the church and in the world. Add to all these outward changes such internal changes in the church as an increasing apparent "worldliness," the changing role of the laity, the new relationships between church and state, and the social reform and spiritual awakening movements, and a picture emerges of a church in ferment. The challenge is to courageously follow God in His plans for His church by obeying His Word and submitting to His Spirit's guidance.

People Movements

Sixth, because in recent years many areas of the world have witnessed a sudden receptivity to the gospel, preparing thousands and thousands of people for membership in the great family of God. Whole villages, tribes, and even countries have become ripe for the harvest: Brazil, Indonesia, Burundi, and Bolivia, to mention only a few. Such people movements challenge us to rethink our goal and practice of mission and to make the necessary preparation to accommodate them. We must ever remember that the last events in the mission of God will be unprecedentedly rapid and extensive.

One idea that deserves greater attention, therefore, is that today—and in the near future—we should invest more money where the harvest truly is ripe and being reaped, instead of continuing to spend our funds on fields where the Holy Spirit has not yet prepared harvest. Failure to do this will lead to a disproportionate investment of money and personnel in institutions and areas whose potential and function for the missionary outreach of the church are minimal, while those with much greater missionary potential will suffer irredeemable loss.

Mission is the work of the Holy Spirit. And as He once prevented Paul and Timothy from delivering the message in the province of Asia and from entering Bithynia (Acts 16:7, 8), so the Spirit, in the same way, challenges His church today. He has already prepared certain areas in the world for harvest, and He challenges us to go there now. There is where we must spend more of our money and dispatch more of our personnel. Tomorrow the Spirit will lead us to other fields.

As a world church the Adventist Church cannot be guided by geographical, organizational, or ecclesiastical-institutional boundaries, nor by business principles developed by Ford Motor Company. The coming decade will witness many more tribes, villages, and nations suddenly becoming greatly receptive to the gospel. Thousands and thousands of people will have to be harvested at the same time. This tremendous challenge should awaken the church so that it will be prepared wherever and whenever these people movements arise.

New Methods

Because of the new situation in the world, in Christendom in general, and in the Adventist Church in particular, we must develop new forms of mission, new methods, and new strategies. The danger of merely perpetuating certain established institutions and tested programs looms very large in our generation of continuous and rapid change. Mission could thus stagnate and opportunities wane. The challenge of mission today, then, is for the church to develop new forms and methods of mission that will stimulate and help implement its missionary role.[3]

The need, really, demands a *multiform structure of the church in mission*. This may mean, on the one hand, that certain institutions and programs which once greatly stimulated the mission of the church may have to be abandoned because they no longer perform that function. The church may have to develop new forms that will follow the missionary function. On the other hand, it may mean that certain institutions and programs which in one area of the world greatly contribute to the success of mission do not perform that role in other areas. Promoting such institutions there would mean not only wasted money, effort, and time, but also disobedience to our great calling.

There is nothing sacrosanct about ecclesiastical forms and structures. They are only temporary—necessary, but temporary—means to a goal. The only criterion, therefore, is whether they enable us to engage with the world of our time in the missionary outreach of the church. Thus, a critical self-examination is urgently needed to determine whether our hospitals, our schools, our liturgy, our methods of evangelism, and our organizational structures really are contributing to the missionary dimension of the church.

It is not at all imaginary that in certain fields the church may have to abandon some of its hospitals, schools, departments, ecclesiastical boundaries, etc. We should not look upon such a need as a failure but rather as the successful completion of a task, opening the way for greater outreach. I pray that the church will have the insight and the faith, the humility and the courage, to adjust itself to the new challenges and situations that will hasten Christ's coming.

The Bridegroom Is Delayed

All this is even more imperative since the Adventist Church stands in danger of losing its missionary fervor and true pilgrim nature as a result of the delay in Christ's coming. As a result, more and more issues of leisure and pleasure are becoming a problem in the life of the church and are requiring a disproportionate amount of attention on the part of its leaders and administrators. Such issues, for sure, have always formed part of the church, but they have remained in their proper perspective. Discipline constituted part of making disciples for Christ, not a separate issue as it is becoming now.

The same holds true about the doctrinal debates regarding the essence of the church and its mission, creationism, or the authority of Ellen G. White's writings. There must be room for doctrinal discussion—without it the church would never fulfill its ongoing mission in a revolutionary world—but doctrinal debates, like in the early Christian church and in the early Adventist Church, should be part of the church's missionary effort to win men to Christ. When the debates become an issue in themselves, it is a danger sign of a church losing its urgency of mission, as the whole history of mission bears out.

The Safe Path

The answers to these challenges which our "third- and fourth-generation church" faces lie in the *clarity of our concept of mission, its relevance to the world,* and our *personal commitment.* So does our success in mission. Ellen G. White summarized these basic challenges of mission today in these well-known words: "The varying circumstances taking place in our world call for labor which will meet these peculiar develop-

ments. The Lord has need of men who are spiritually sharp and clear-sighted. . . . Upon the minds of such, God's Word flashes light, revealing to them more than ever before the safe path." [4]

Ellen White warned, therefore, never to reject out of hand what has never been taught. "Away with these restrictions. . . . That which God gives His servants to speak today would not perhaps have been present truth twenty years ago, but it is God's message for this time." [5] "Present truth, from the first letter of its alphabet to the last, means missionary effort." [6]

The Answer

The following chapters speak to these challenges. What will be our answer? Never before has a generation of Christians known greater potential, resourcefulness, power, and opportunity than ours. Neither has there been a more urgent time.

The average per capita income in the U.S. is some $4,000, by far the highest in the world. How are American Adventists using their money? The history of mission recounts human misappropriations of talents, money, and other gifts. Yet, when God sends His church certain gifts, He always has in mind the whole world. One answer to the challenge of mission today, therefore, lies in the proper stewardship of our money, educational capacities, and technological achievements.

Of course, the riches we share are not confined to our material prosperity, our insights in health and sanitation, or in our achievements of freedom and democracy. No matter how significantly these may serve for the betterment of humanity, the answer to the challenge of mission lies in our riches of faith. Paul's exhortation, "Examine yourselves: are you living the life of faith?" (2 Corinthians 13:5), perennially challenges every Christian. God has chosen "those who are poor in the eyes of the world to be rich in faith and to inherit the kingdom he has promised to those who love him," the Apostle James assures us. (James 2:5.)

How deep, really, is this conviction of our faith in God and our love to Him?

Mission is personal. Programs and institutions will never accomplish it of themselves. God's mission is fulfilled as *Incarnation,* and it will make our mission possible: Christ living and working in us. (Galatians 2:20; John 17:26; Philippians 4:13.) Mission is possible only if Christ dwells in us, motivates us, and speaks through us. (2 Corinthians 5:20; John 16:1-12.) Only when He lives in us, will we have genuine humility and self-denial, patience and perseverance, consecration and obedience, and, above all, love.

Do we recognize that Christ dwells in us? (2 Corinthians 13: 5.) Then we shall experience the "unspeakable joy" of participating with Him in mission: becoming an Asian with the Asians, a black with the blacks, poor with the poor, and oppressed with the oppressed, as He did.

[1] Ellen G. White, *The Desire of Ages* (Mountain View, California: Pacific Press Publishing Association, 1940), p. 822.

[2] *Ibid.,* p. 195.

[3] Ellen G. White, *Gospel Workers* (Battle Creek, Michigan: Review and Herald Publishing Co., 1892), p. 294.

[4] Ellen G. White, Manuscript 8a, 1888, as printed in A. V. Olson, *Through Crisis to Victory, 1888-1901* (Washington, D.C.: Review and Herald Publishing Association, 1966), p. 273.

[5] *Ibid.,* pp. 273, 274.

[6] Ellen G. White, *Counsels on Health* (Mountain View, California: Pacific Press Publishing Association, 1923), p. 300.

Continuity and Change in Adventist Mission

The Seventh-day Adventist Church sprang from the "great second advent awakening," which shook the Christian world in Europe and the Americas in the early nineteenth century, and from the Millerite movement in particular. During the years immediately following the Great Disappointment of 1844, when Christ did not return as the Adventists had expected and when the various mainline churches rejected the Millerite message of Christ's soon coming, a new community of Christians developed with a common body of doctrines. Between 1860 and 1863 the denominational name and basic organization of the Seventh-day Adventist Church were adopted.

The distinguishing doctrines of Seventh-day Adventism include the belief that Christ's second advent is very near, the observance of the seventh day as the Sabbath, Christ's ministry today in the sanctuary in heaven, the immutability of God's Ten Commandment law, and the recognition of Ellen Gould White as a special messenger "sent from God" to guide the movement "through the wilderness to the heavenly Canaan." Her influence on the development, unity, and continuity of the church, its doctrines, and its missionary activities can hardly be overestimated.

Like the Protestant Reformers, such as Luther and Calvin, the early Seventh-day Adventist pioneers believed that the gospel had already been preached in all the world. They also felt that the churches of their day had rejected the special message of Christ's soon return and the preparation it required on man's part. For that reason they confined their particular mission to those converted Christians who already believed in the soon coming of Christ and who had gone through the experience of the Great Disappointment. For a time Ellen G. White also held this view [1] that Christ had forever shut the door of mercy, that He had finished His work for the world. So firmly did many believe this that one early Christian was nearly refused the Seventh-day Adventist message because the individual presenting it doubted the possibility of the salvation of anyone who had not participated in the 1844 movement. [2]

After 1851, however, Adventists gave up this view. Visions given to Ellen G. White during these formative years gradually convinced the early Seventh-day Adventists that they had a message for a much wider circle than those of the original Advent faith. But it took some decades before the new denomination adopted and put into practice this new missionary vision. *This period from 1844 to the early 1850's constitutes the first phase of Seventh-day Adventist mission.*

During the late 1850's and 1860's, the leaders of the new church became convinced that many Christians in North America had not rejected the "three angels' messages of Revelation 14:6-12," as was first believed, but that they merely had never heard about it. The Adventists then came to believe that God had many honest children in the various Christian churches who had to be called out in order to be saved. The church believed that those other churches as corporate bodies had rejected the "last warning message," but that individuals within those apostate churches could still be rescued. *These individual Christians, then, became the object of Seventh-day Adventist mission during the second phase of its mission work.*

In those days the Adventist Church gave little or no thought to expanding its mission work to areas outside North America. To the contrary, early in 1859 a reader of the *Review and Herald* asked the editor, "Is the Third Angel's Message being given, or to be given except in the United States?" to which Uriah Smith answered, "We have no information that the Third Message [sic] is at present being proclaimed in any country besides our own. Analogy would lead us to expect that the proclamation of this message would be co-extensive with the first: though this might not perhaps be necessary to fulfill Rev. x, 11 [sic], since our own land is composed of people from almost every nation." [3]

This last argument was used over and over again. The proclamation of Seventh-day Adventist belief to all nations, tribes, and languages was being fulfilled right in the United States, where the representatives of the whole world lived. In fact, so strongly did many believe this that they discouraged the believers who wanted to go abroad to preach Adventism from doing so. Seventh-day Adventist mission in its second phase was America-centric in outreach, scope, and fulfillment.

Especially among the Adventist immigrants were men who wanted to go back to Europe and proclaim their newfound faith, but church leaders felt that such a policy would waste time and effort and even signify unbelief in Christ's soon coming. One of these immigrants, M. B. Czechowski, was a former Polish Roman Catholic. Since the Seventh-day Adventist leaders strongly advised him not to return to Europe, this determined missionary applied to another denomination, which sent him to Europe in 1864. Czechowski preached in northern Italy, Switzerland, southern Germany, and even eastern Europe, establishing several independent companies of Seventh-day Adventist believers.

"By accident" these groups heard about the newly organized church in North America and contacted it in 1869, which eventually led to the sending of J. N. Andrews as the first Seventh-day Adventist missionary from North America in September, 1874. Earlier that same year the first issue of the *True Missionary*, a magazine urging Seventh-day Adventists to send out missionaries to other countries, had appeared. *The year 1874 marks the beginning of the third phase of Seventh-day Adventist mission, in which the Adventist Church expanded geographically into all the world. It burst its North American bounds.*

Go Therefore . . .

Four factors will significantly contribute to an understanding of the Adventist mission as it began to develop in the 1870's.

First, the early Adventist leaders continued to believe that the gospel had already been preached "in all the world" and that the world was, by and large, a Christian world. They often quoted Christ's prophecy in Matthew 24:14, "This gospel of the kingdom shall be preached in all the world, . . . and then shall the end come" (K.J.V.), as a prominent sign of the last days, which, they felt, had been fulfilled in the worldwide expansion of Protestant missions. In the April 16, 1872, issue of the *Review and Herald,* D. M. Canright, for instance, quoted other writers who had stated that "the whole heathen world is dotted with missions. . . . Three-fourths of the earth's surface is under Christian government and influence," and "the missionaries that have been, now for half a century, at work have leavened almost every quarter of the globe." He remarked, "This looks very much as though the above prophecy [Matthew 24:14] were about fulfilled." [4]

Second, Adventists considered themselves a movement within Christendom and its "last remnant." They felt that the mainline churches had willfully rejected the three angels' messages and that the Seventh-day Adventist missionary's task was to call the honest children of God out of "Babylon." These honest individuals became the object of Adventist mission. Thus, when Adventist missionaries left the shores of North America in this third phase of Seventh-day Adventist mission, they all went to Christian countries and people: Switzerland (1874), Germany (1875), France (1876), Italy (1877), Denmark (1877), Norway (1878), England (1879), and Australia (1885).

The Adventist Church expanded its work among the Christian populations of the world, paying almost no attention to the much larger non-Christian world. It simply had no room for the Muslim, the Hindu, the Buddhist, etc., in its concept of the impending conflict between the powers of good and evil, which deals especially with an apostate Christian world. When Seventh-day Adventism gradually expanded its work to the former colonial areas, its missionaries commonly approached the foreigners first—colonial administrators, settlers, and business people—and then the indigenous population, notably the Christians among them. Understandably, this missionary concept and strategy has often branded Adventists as "sheep stealers."

In fact, Adventist missionaries really did not expect a great harvest from the "decadent and corrupt organizations, called Babylon." [5] When, in the 1920's, A. G. Daniells remarked at a workers' meeting that sound evangelistic preaching would prepare millions whom Jesus would save at His second coming, not a few ministers expressed their doubts about his orthodoxy.

Third, not only did Seventh-day Adventist mission work and message presuppose the existence of a Christian church, it also presupposed the ability to read. In a large number of countries Adventist mission work began and developed through denominational publications. Adventists have, therefore, rightly called their publishing work "the legs of the message." Consequently, although Adventists have done more than any other mission organization to establish a worldwide system of schools, the large percentage of illiterates in the world, mostly non-Christians, have remained the forgotten half of Seventh-day Adventist evangelism.

Fourth, the first Seventh-day Adventist overseas missionary went because the overseas fields urgently and insistently requested him. And like the first three factors, which for decades have shaped the Adventist concept and strategy of mission, this last factor has remained characteristic of its mission from the beginning. Adventist missionaries go overseas to assist the believers in their work, making the overseas fields the determining factor of mission, rather than the sending organization.

When J. N. Andrews, the Adventists' first missionary, set foot in Europe, he conceived of his mission, according to his letter to the General Conference, printed in the Review and Herald of November 24, 1874, as preaching the Sabbath, warning the people of the coming judgment, and calling God's people to obey His unchangeable law.[6] This, then, constituted the special message for Adventists to proclaim to Christian believers all over the world. Truly the Advent Movement in those days tended toward legalism and self-righteousness. And since it believed that these truths set people free, its whole emphasis of missionary preaching lay in "presenting the doctrines." Christ and His love for sinners were not sufficiently prominent in Adventist evangelistic preaching and religious literature.

Ellen G. White constantly criticized this narrow concept of the church and its mission. She never tired of emphasizing over and over again that "the burden of our message should be the mission and life of Jesus Christ. Let there be a dwelling upon the humiliation, self-denial, meekness, and lowliness of Christ. . . . Show to your hearers Jesus in His condescension to save fallen man." [7]

"By many who have been engaged in the work for this time, Christ has been made secondary, and theories and arguments have had first place. . . . They have not had views of Jesus, and have not proclaimed the fact that, where sin abounded, grace doth much more abound. . . . What a loss it is to the soul who understands the strong claims of the law, and who yet fails to understand the grace of Christ which doth much more abound!" [8]

She spoke of sadly neglected subjects upon which Adventists should have dwelt: that God loves the world, that righteousness is by faith, and that man is saved by grace.[9]

Adventism had become too dependent on the impregnability of its doctrinal position and stood in danger of losing its relationship with Christ.[10] Ellen G. White, clearly seeing this danger, guided the church to higher ground. She saw that religion did not consist of a system of dry doctrines [11] and said, "There is danger of . . . dwelling too much on doctrines." [12] Doctrines will never lead persons to Christ, for "the observance of external forms will never meet the great want of the human soul." [13] Present Christ—Christ nailed to the cross. "And when the people behold Christ as He is, they will not wrangle over doctrines." [14] The main question is, "Do we have faith in Christ?" [15]

This continuous emphasis on "Christ as the burden of our message" gradually won a hearing among the leaders of the church. The legalism of the first and second phases of Adventist mission and the rather narrow concept of the church as a doctrinal system haltingly made room for the vision that salvation is by grace through faith and not by works of the law. The General Conference session of 1888 in Minneapolis is a famous milestone on this way to a deeper understanding of the Adventist missionary message to the world.

The new missionary outreach after 1874 not only affected Seventh-day Adventist theology, but also led to a total reorganization of the structure of the church. The reorganization of 1901 and 1903 still stands today as an exemplary model of church missionary structure. The rigid vertical organization in churches, conferences, and General Conference prior to 1901 was not suited for the missionary advance of the church. It had caused immobility and stagnation. A few leaders at the top marked out and controlled every aspect of the work, sometimes in its minutest detail.[16]

Ellen G. White continually urged for a change, emphasizing more decentralization and greater responsibilities for men and institutions in their respective fields and endeavors of work. Most of these counsels came from her pen while she served

in various mission fields outside North America. As in her message on legalism and the too narrow concept of the church, she uplifted Christ as the model of earthly structures: "Jesus is to superintend all events in the present and future of His church. . . . Oh, that men would revere the great head of the church, and would manufacture less human methods. . . . He says to everyone holding a position of trust, 'Learn of me; for I am meek and lowly in heart.' "[17]

One of Adventism's greatest pioneer missionaries, A. G. Daniells, with holy boldness dared to suggest at the beginning of the General Conference of 1901 that the usual rules and precedents for arranging and transacting the business of the conference be suspended. "We will throw away our preconceived opinions, and will step out boldly to follow the light that he gives us, whether we can see clear through to the end or not,—if we walk in the light we have, . . . God will give us further light. . . . He will not lead us into confusion, brethren. He will lead us into order, . . . that he himself establishes, and . . . in no way circumscribe or hinder his work, but will carry it forward with power and great rapidity. . . . May God help us for his own name's sake." [18] All previous plans for the business of the conference were laid aside, and the work of reorganization was begun.

The church, at that time, required a greater horizontal organization to advance the work. The danger, of course, was to swing the pendulum too far the other way, as was the case with most other missionary societies. However, the outcome of the conference, under the Holy Spirit's guidance, marvelously combined a vertical structure with horizontal organization (departments within divisions, unions, etc.), which other churches have admired ever since. A. G. Daniells was elected president and for the next twenty years led out in a mission program that has not had its equal since the early Christians conquered the world.

During those twenty years the Seventh-day Adventist mission expanded over the whole globe. Up to Daniells' election as president, only one or two Adventist missionaries had been sent out from North America every year. The year following his election the Seventh-day Adventist Church sent sixty new missionaries overseas, and during his whole presidency ninety new Adventist missionaries, on the average, left the shores of North America every year.

It certainly is not sheer coincidence that Daniells also wrote the well-known book *Christ Our Righteousness*, which opens with this statement: "Christ our righteousness is the one sublime message set forth in the Sacred Scriptures." [19] This gradually became the leading motto during these years of rapid and phenomenal expansion. Success in mission is always closely related to the particular message proclaimed and lived out.

J. N. Loughborough summed up Daniells' work of bold reorganization at the 1901 General Conference in these words: "When we have heeded the light that he [God] has given, the cause has gone straight every time; and the difficulties in the way have been when we have not strictly heeded the instruction that God has given." [20]

The rapid expansion of the Seventh-day Adventist missionary movement over the whole earth not only stimulated the reorganization of the structure of the church and a reformulation of its message, but also led to a different self-understanding. During the first and second phases of its mission, the Adventist Church mainly conceived of itself as a *doctrinal body* to keep, guard, and proclaim "the truth." Becoming a member was expressed in the term "accepting the truth," and being a church member was "being in the truth." They conceived of the Adventist Church as a *way to salvation*—"walk ye therein." In the third phase of Adventist mission, this concept gave way to the larger concept of the church as the *body of Christ.* But another danger threatened, namely, the tendency to conceive of the "body of Christ" as a holy, prestigious institution. While they laid less emphasis on doctrinal positions, Adventists still stood in as much danger of self-righteousness as in the first two phases.

As time went by, the church tended to glory in itself as an institution of God, boasting of its great accomplishments: its sound financial basis (124 million dollars in tithe, 16.5 million in Sabbath School offerings, 10.5 million in other offerings for world missions, plus 60 million for local funds in 1970—a total of 210 million dollars each year

and a total investment of over a billion dollars); its number of schools (some 4,600), hospitals (139), and clinics (152); and its growing influence, prestige, and good name. The church as an institution tended to become an *ark of salvation,* replacing the *way of salvation* suggested by the church as a doctrinal system.

Ellen G. White, who by her visions guided Adventists past the Scylla of the first phases of its mission, also clearly warned of the Charybdis of this latter phase. "The zealous cry may be heard, 'The temple of the Lord, The temple of the Lord, are these!' " "The steady progress of our work and our increased facilities are filling the hearts and minds of many of our people with satisfaction and pride, which we fear will take the place of the love of God in the soul." [21] Adventist mission was, to a large extent, church-centered.

Into All the World

Since the late 1950's the Seventh-day Adventist Church has entered the fourth and, hopefully, the last phase of its mission. The impetus to this new phase again came from the expanding work of overseas mission. In their push to the remotest ends of the earth as Christ had commanded, Adventist missionaries discovered millions upon millions of people who had never even heard of Christ. In fact, *about 80 percent of the whole world population is non-Christian.* The first three phases of Adventist mission allowed hardly any room for these non-Christians in its missionary thinking, but today the non-Christian world has gradually begun to loom very large. Moreover, in the mission field Adventist missionaries came into close contact with other Christian missionary organizations, which they learned to respect as also fulfilling a definite role in God's plan of salvation.

All this has led to a shift of emphasis in the Seventh-day Adventist missionary message and to a different concept of the church and its mission. J. N. Andrews could define the essence of the three angels' messages as "preach the Sabbath, warn of the coming judgment, and teach obedience to the commandments," but now it has a different emphasis. M. K. Eckenroth has written in *Our Firm Foundation:* Conversion,

the cross, and the love of Christ are the center of the three angels' messages.[22] Apparently Seventh-day Adventist doctrines have now found their proper relationship to Christ, the center of all doctrine.

Adventists have begun to rediscover that "the present truth presents Christ, not only humiliated and crucified, but risen and glorified. It holds up Christ as our exemplar while upon earth, our advocate above, and our approaching king in the world to come. It points to Christ as the only means of escape from eternal death, and to his second coming as the blessed hope of the people of God in all ages." [23]

A number of studies appearing in recent years have clearly illustrated this shift of emphasis —Otto Gmehling's *Christ the Lord in the Beliefs and Life of Seventh-day Adventists,* H. M. S. Richards' *What Jesus Said,* and M. K. Eckenroth's *Christ the Center of Our Preaching.* The world in general has clearly recognized this trend, and Walter Martin and D. G. Barnhouse have concluded, therefore, that "Seventh-day Adventists are a truly Christian group." [24] Indeed, Seventh-day Adventists have finally come to where Ellen G.

White wanted them to be: "The burden of our message should be the mission and life of Jesus Christ." [25]

In the first, second, and third phases emphasis was on the *warning* aspect of the Adventist message, which of course presupposed the existence of Christianity wherever its missionaries went. Adventist missionaries, in general, were not prepared to reach out into the non-Christian world. And even still some 90 percent of Adventism's new converts come from a Christian background.

Only now are Seventh-day Adventists beginning to rediscover that their mission involves salvation first, for every person. Only now are they really beginning to discover the world—the whole world—as the true object of their mission, because the world was the object of God's love and God's own mission. This is the world of both jungles and modern megalopolises, of both wealth and poverty, of the classes and the masses, of Animism and Hinduism, of militant Buddhism and crusading Islam, of both secular unbelief and nominal, Spiritless Christianity. For the first time Seventh-day Adventist mission is truly becoming a *world mission.*

Signs abound that God is really ushering in this new phase with its salvation message now. In North America, Adventists have taken a new interest in inner-city work. Its recent mission magazines are full of reports of Buddhist and Muslim converts. In Singapore and Beirut, Adventists, in 1961 and 1963, held the first three conferences for denominational workers among Muslims. A new emphasis is also being laid on Seventh-day Adventist contact with Jewish people, as the founding of the Hebrew Scripture Association in 1955—the forerunner of the Israelite Heritage Institute (1964)—evidenced. The establishment of a department of mission at the Seventh-day Adventist Theological Seminary in 1966 and the General Conference Institute of World Mission for the orientation and training of missionaries, which started that same year, are other important signs of a new era.

With "the burden of our message the mission and life of Jesus Christ" and "the whole world as our parish," there has also gradually developed a deeper understanding of the church and its relationship to God's own mission. During the third phase, the idea of the church as a doctrinal body gave way, not without resistance, to the larger concept of the church as the body of Christ. But then, the concept of the church as the incarnation of God's mission in the world was threatened with obscurity by an emphasis upon the form over the essence—the institution became all important. This danger still remains very much alive. Church and mission, ministry and authority, are still very much identified with its institutional form.

Yet under the impetus of the new insights gained from overseas mission and the Christ-centeredness of the Adventist message, this *church-centrism* of the third phase is gradually making room for a new and genuine *Christ-centrism.* Here lies one of the greatest challenges of Adventist mission in the 1970's. Just as the doctrines have value only in a proper relationship to Christ, so also does the church as an institution.

Today, Seventh-day Adventists define the essence of the church as *"Jesus Christ existing in the minds, or hearts, of those who have accepted Him as their Saviour, who love Him and one another, and who obey His Word as they understand it."* [26] This means that the criterion, really, for belonging to God's church is the person of Jesus Christ. Seventh-day Adventists "do not believe that they alone constitute the true children of God today." [27] To the contrary, with the criterion of the true church being Jesus Christ—His mission, His life, and His faith—the great body of Christ's true followers are found in other Christian communions: [28] Roman Catholic, Orthodox, or Protestant. The perfect fulfillment of Revelation 14: 8, "Fallen, fallen is Babylon the great, she who has made all nations drink the fierce wine of her fornication," is yet future.[29]

The universal church, the one flock under the Good Shepherd, lives in different folds. (John 10: 16.) Each mission society that lifts up Christ before men fulfills part of the divine plan for the evangelization of the world.[30] Seventh-day Adventists believe that their unique part in God's mission is to announce to the whole world that Christ is coming and that all should be ready to meet Him. (Amos 3:7; 4:12; Revelation 14:6-12.) [31] It is not just a warning message—it is saving good news.

Mission: Possible

Such self-understanding has grown progressively deeper with the passing years since the days when the Adventist pioneers first accepted Christ's commission. It ought to become much more the common property of all Seventh-day Adventists in order to make mission in the 70's really successful. And the growing number of signs that indicate the beginning of this new concept of the church is very encouraging.

In their mission to the world, Adventists now cooperate with other Christian denominations in the work of Bible translation, the promotion of religious liberty, in church aid and Christian education, and in many other forms of all-Christian concern. Recent Adventist theological publications reflect the same trend. Over against the strongly apologetic and polemic literature of the first and second phases of Adventist mission now stands the emphasis on Biblical-theological studies, devotional literature, and the common theological heritage they share with the Christian church at large.[32] A similar trend is obvious in Seventh-day Adventist religious magazines.

All these characteristics of this fourth phase of Adventist mis-sion, however, will ultimately culminate in the greatest one of all: the gathering of people from all nations—the remnant—to meet their Lord. The *unprecedented growth of the church* indicates the first happy fruits of this great harvest. The problems arising from this rapid growth resemble those at the end of the last century, which led to the reorganization of the structure of the church. A similar restructuring has become even more urgent today, now that already over 80 percent of the Adventist membership lives outside North America. The era of Europe is over, and the era of Asia has begun.

The church has already taken the first small steps, and, hopefully, God will now raise up men like Elder Daniells, men who willingly and daringly say, "We will throw away our preconceived opinions, and will step out boldly to follow the light that he gives us, whether we can see clear through to the end or not."[33]

A New Testament Parallel

This bird's-eye view of the development of Adventist missionary thinking reveals striking similarities to the early Christian church. We would do well to remind ourselves of these parallels in order to better understand God's leading of the Advent Movement as well as to silence those critics in and outside the church who keep pointing at "inconsistencies" between past and present positions.

Let us look for a moment at Jesus' own concept of mission. Did He not clearly state that He had come for the Israelites alone? (Matthew 15:24.) He Himself never set foot outside of Palestine, and He never learned a language other than His own. During His lifetime He explicitly forbade His disciples to go to other than their own people. (Matthew 10:5, 6.) From the records it seems that Jesus did not even expect that His disciples would accomplish their mission before His return. (Matthew 10:23.) Did Jesus Himself, then, never intend any mission to the Gentiles, as some contend? Would that mission perhaps be fulfilled in the heathen coming to Israel as in the Old Testament view of mission? Or would God in the last days send someone else to the Gentiles?

None of these. The New Testa- ment teaches very clearly that Jesus' work included all the world. It, however, needed a definite beginning in one place before it could be expanded to include all nations, tribes, and tongues. Therefore, the restriction to one place and the exclusiveness were necessary. A congregation must first be formed, firmly established, and instructed in the Word by the Lord before He can use it as an instrument of His great mission. This is exactly what happened with Jesus' disciples, with the early Christian church, and with the great Advent Movement.

The gospel must be understood, believed, and lived out in its fullness before men can go out and teach others. This always calls, at first, for an exclusive group with a limited assignment that gradually expands in concentric circles. Jesus called His disciples as representatives of all Israel, trained them, instructed them, and then sent them out—but not immediately —in all directions unto the remotest ends of the earth. So after Jesus' ascension, He spoke to the new congregation, a representation of all people on earth, of Jerusalem first, and then, like concentric circles, of Judea, Samaria, and the far ends of the earth.

The history of mission clearly shows that when the gospel spreads too rapidly—without a proper organization which guards the Biblical truth and which follows up its proclamation—distortions, falsehoods, and misinterpretations result. For this very r e a s o n God, at times, had to prevent His own followers from expanding into certain areas or from going too quickly. Jesus' own disciples experienced this, and so did Paul and Barnabas, who "were prevented by the Holy Spirit from delivering the message in the province of Asia." (Acts 16:6.)

The development of the missionary idea among Seventh-day Adventists evidences this leading of God. Adventism's first phase of mission corresponds closely to that of Jesus' disciples in the beginning of their calling and to that of the early church following the resurrection. They had to "stay in Jerusalem and Judea." For Adventists, an organization had to develop and become established (1844-1863). Early Seventh-day Adventist leaders had to understand clearly and fully the nature of the mission for which God was preparing them. When the commission came, they accepted it with the same sense of urgency as the disciples and the Apostle Paul. They felt strongly convinced that Christ would come during their lifetime. They said, "Now is the time that the kingdom is being established. There is no time left. Perhaps there will not be enough time to go to all the places even in North America." (Cf. Matthew 10:23.)

Why smile about this urgency? It is Biblical. It betrays genuine faith. Neither should we underestimate the great expansion of the Protestant missionary movement at that time. When John Mott led his Student Christian Movement into all the world under the motto, "The evangelization of all the world in this generation," they were all convinced that it was possible. Under this sense of urgency, thousands of Protestant missionaries spread the gospel to all the countries of the world at the turn of the century. The percentage of the world's population which was Christian rose from 18 percent in 1820 to 30 percent in 1900 and was rapidly increasing in the first decade of this century. Early Adventists considered the

Continuity and Change in Adventist Mission

Seventh-day Adventist communion of believers a prophetic movement *within* this rapidly expanding worldwide Christian church. They called the believers to obedience to God and sought to prepare themselves for the imminent end. (Matthew 24:14.)

But then, rather abruptly, the Protestant missionary movement lost its momentum and ground to a halt. The Protestant message lost its clarity, certainty, and urgency. Reports from those days describe the tragic results in many mission areas of the world. The percentage of Christians in the world dropped from 40 percent in the first decade of this century to barely 20 percent in 1971. Churches deserted their faith and the missionary spirit. A mass apostasy affected so many of them that today some 1,600 million people have never even heard about Christ. Another billion people have never heard Seventh-day Adventism's message clearly. A whole new task awaits the A d v e n t i s t Church: To go to all the world, Christian and non-Christian.

In This Generation

Ellen G. White and other early Adventists believed they saw the fulfillment of prophecies in Christianity's turning away from the eternal gospel and the belief in Christ's second coming, which in earlier years had stimulated the great Protestant missionary movement. In no uncertain terms did the Adventist leaders denounce the situation of these "apostate" Protestant churches. However, the future was still veiled to them. God in His mercy and patience restrained the powers of evil from taking full control of this world and His churches.

The enemy has taken a seat in the temple of God, claiming to be a god himself (2 Thessalonians 2:3, 4), and we know that the secret power of wickedness is already very much at work today (verses 5-10). However, the "falling away" from Christ has not yet reached its culmination. Since the early 1960's, a whole new missionary zeal has gripped many of the evangelical churches. Again, as a century ago, many hundreds of missionaries are leaving the shores of America every year to assist in the work of harvesting overseas.

This new missionary spirit was born among the churches of the Third World, and there it is affecting the Christian church most strongly. In Africa, for instance, the number of Christians has increased from thirty-five million in the early 1950's to a hundred million in 1971. Whereas in the West the percentage of professing Christians is rapidly decreasing, in the Third World the number of Christians is tripling every twenty years. Since 1967 large regional congresses on evangelism have been held in Berlin, Singapore, Bogotá, Minneapolis, Mexico City, and other places. Just as a hundred years ago, so today calls are ringing everywhere to "evangelize the whole world in this generation." But, unlike a century ago, the center of this evangelistic thrust and its leadership has come from the Christian churches in Africa, Asia, and Latin America.

As yet we do not fully know the consequences of this new pattern for Christianity. For the Adventist Church, however, it means taking more seriously than ever before the recognition that God also has other agencies in the world to evangelize the whole world in this generation. Therefore *conscientious cooperation* in this worldwide evangelistic thrust is imperative.

The great task of cooperating with other churches in evangelizing the non-Christian population should not detract, however, from the original cause of Adventist mission: calling with a loud voice to Christians and non-Christians alike to live out the faith of Jesus, to keep His commandments, and to ready themselves for the day of Christ's soon return. Seventh-day Adventists can never leave to others what God has entrusted to them.

With the great body of Christ's true followers in the other Christian communions [34] and with God daily adding thousands of new converts to this worldwide Christian community, the greatest challenge to the Advent Movement now is to cooperate with the Holy Spirit in gathering God's "remnant" (Revelation 12:17) from all nations and religions to prepare for the Lord's coming.

[1] Ellen G. White, *Selected Messages,* Book One (Washington, D.C.: Review and Herald Publishing Association, 1958), pp. 63, 64.

[2] J. H. Waggoner and others, "Conference Address," *Advent Review and Sabbath Herald,* June 11, 1861, p. 21. The others were: James White, J. N. Loughborough, E. W. Shortridge, Joseph Bates, J. B. Frisbe, M. E. Cornell, Moses Hull,

and John Byington.

[3] A. W. Spalding, *Origin and History of Seventh-day Adventists,* Vol. 2 (Captains of the Host, revised; Washington, D.C.: Review and Herald Publishing Association, 1962), p. 194.

[4] D. M. Canright, "Present Condition of the World," *Advent Review and Herald of the Sabbath,* April 16, 1872, p. 138.

[5] A. W. Spalding, *Christ's Last Legion* (Washington, D.C.: Review and Herald Publishing Association, 1949), p. 715.

[6] J. N. Andrews, "Meeting of Sabbath-keepers in Neuchatel," *Advent Review and Herald of the Sabbath,* November 24, 1874, p. 172.

[7] Ellen G. White, "The Work of the Minister," *Advent Review and Sabbath Herald,* September 11, 1888, p. 578.

[8] White, *Selected Messages,* Book One, pp. 383, 384.

[9] Ellen G. White, *Testimonies for the Church,* Vol. 4 (Mountain View, California: Pacific Press Publishing Association, 1948), pp. 371-383.

[10] N. F. Pease, "The Gospel in Early Adventism," *Review and Herald,* September 4, 1969, p. 3.

[11] White, *Testimonies,* Vol. 4, pp. 375-378.

[12] Ellen G. White, *Counsels to Writers and Editors* (Nashville, Tennessee: Southern Publishing Association, 1946), p. 79; see also, Ellen G. White, *Gospel Workers* (1892), pp. 39-47.

[13] Ellen G. White, "Unity of the Church," *Advent Review and Sabbath Herald,* January 25, 1887, p. 49.

[14] Ellen G. White, *Colporteur Ministry* (Mountain View, California: Pacific Press Publishing Association, 1953), p. 49.

[15] White, *Gospel Workers,* pp. 429-433.

[16] Ellen G. White, *Testimonies to Min-isters and Gospel Workers* (Battle Creek, Michigan: Review and Herald Publishing Co., 1893), pp. 301-303; Ellen G. White, Manuscript 43, 1895, as printed in A. V. Olson, *Through Crisis to Victory, 1888-1901,* p. 162.

[17] Olson, *Through Crisis to Victory,* pp. 164, 165.

[18] A. G. Daniells, *General Conference Bulletin,* April 3, 1901, p. 27.

[19] A. G. Daniells, *Christ Our Righteousness* (Washington, D.C.: Review and Herald Publishing Association, 1941), p. 9.

[20] J. N. Loughborough, *General Conference Bulletin,* April 25, 1901, p. 460.

[21] White, *Gospel Workers,* p. 37.

[22] M. K. Eckenroth, "Christ the Center of All True Preaching," *Our Firm Foundation,* Vol. 1 (Washington, D.C.: Review and Herald Publishing Association, 1953), p. 156.

[23] G. C. Tenney, "Preaching Christ," *Advent Review and Sabbath Herald,* September 16, 1880, p. 201.

[24] Walter R. Martin, *The Truth About Seventh-day Adventism* (Grand Rapids, Michigan: Zondervan Publishing House, 1960), p. 7.

[25] White, "The Work of the Minister," *Review and Herald,* September 11, 1888, p. 578.

[26] "Nature of the Church," *Seventh-day Adventist Encyclopedia,* Commentary Reference Series, Vol. 10 (Washington, D.C.: Review and Herald Publishing Association, 1966), p. 266. (Italics supplied.)

[27] *Ibid.,* p. 267.

[28] Ellen G. White, *The Great Controversy Between Christ and Satan* (Mountain View, California: Pacific Press Publishing Association, 1911), p. 390.

[29] *Ibid.,* p. 604.

[30] *Seventh-day Adventists Answer*

Questions on Doctrine (Washington, D.C.: Review and Herald Publishing Association, 1957), pp. 625, 626. This book was prepared by a group of S.D.A. leaders, Bible teachers, and editors.

[31] *Ibid.,* p. 627.

[32] Compare with L. E. Froom's works: *The Prophetic Faith of Our Fathers* (4 vols.; Washington, D.C.: Review and Herald Publishing Association, 1946-54); and *The Conditionalist Faith of Our Fathers* (2 vols.; Washington, D.C.: Review and Herald Publishing Association, 1966, 1965).

[33] Daniells, *Bulletin,* April 3, 1901, p. 27.

[34] White, *The Great Controversy,* p. 390.

Seventh-day Adventist Mission in the Seventies

Three features stand out most prominently in the present missionary situation of the Seventh-day Adventist Church.

First, the church has been planted over the whole globe and *is now the most widespread single Protestant denomination, working in 84 percent of all countries.*[1] Praise and gratitude go to our Lord, the "missionary-in-chief,"[2] who has worked this miracle in less than a century. Such a rapid and far-reaching expansion has not had its equal since the early Christian church conquered the world. It provides the clearest evidence that all mission is God's work. Continually reminding themselves of how God has led in the past, Adventists should worry very little about the continuing future of their mission. Now that the gospel has reached the remotest ends of the world, we have truly entered the very last days of this world's history. (Matthew 24:14.)

Second, with the growth of Adventism, *the larger portion of its membership lives outside North America and the Western World in general.* (See Figure 1.) Until the early 1950's the majority of Adventists lived in North America, Europe, and Australia. Since the late 1950's, however, this picture has suddenly and radically changed. In Latin America, Africa, and Asia nothing less than a church explosion has taken place, and it will continue in the 1970's.

43

FIGURE 1
Percentages of Adventist World Membership

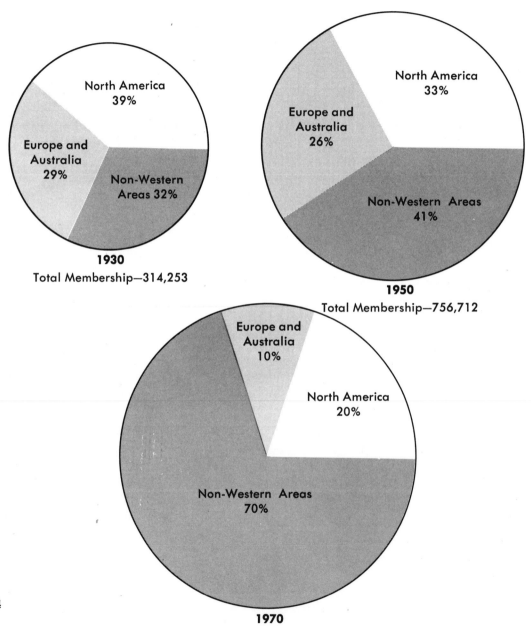

North America
39%

Europe and
Australia
29%

Non-Western
Areas 32%

1930
Total Membership—314,253

North America
33%

Europe and
Australia
26%

Non-Western Areas
41%

1950
Total Membership—756,712

Europe and
Australia
10%

North America
20%

Non-Western Areas
70%

1970
Total Membership—c. 2,000,000

As a result, only 20 percent of the Adventist world membership now lives in the United States, where the church originated. The annual growth rate in North America is less than 2 percent, and in Europe and Australia it ranges similarly from minus 1 percent to 3 percent. In fact, only because of the present high growth rate of the Adventist Church in Latin America and Africa—9 to 15 percent a year—is the Seventh-day Adventist Church as a whole still growing at a rate of about 5 percent a year. (See Figure 2.)

We may expect, as a result, that by the end of this decade Adventist membership in North America will make up barely 10 percent of the total world membership. This means that the Seventh-day Adventist Church, much more than Christendom in general, in the seventies will become largely a non-Western, nonwhite church. Because of its high percentage of first-generation believers, however, the Adventist Church will remain a very viable and active church. It may be expected that these members in Latin America, Africa, and Asia will have an increasingly revitalizing influence on the Adventist Church as a whole and on its missionary outreach in the seventies. And the prospect of the development of an Asian, African, and Latin American force of overseas missionaries will become one of the greatest assets to Seventh-day Adventist world mission in the seventies.

Third, *the scope of the unfinished task is immense.* At Christ's birth, there were 200 million people in the world. Some 1,800 years later, by the time the General Conference of Seventh-day Adventists was organized, the world population had reached its first billion mark. Today there are 3.8 billion people in the world, a number which will have increased to 5.5 billion by the end of the seventies.

Today, as noted before, barely 20 percent of the world population is Christian. Moreover, this 20 percent is very unevenly distributed. Of all Roman Catholics, for instance, some 90 percent live in Europe and North and Latin America, but 80 percent of the world population does not live there. Protestants show a similar distribution. About 80 percent of all Protestants live among 25 percent of the world population. The Seventh-day Adventist Church has done a little

FIGURE 2
Percentage Increase of Adventist World Membership, 1968-69

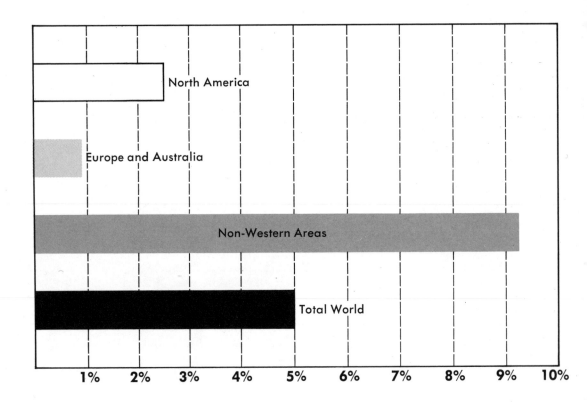

North America

Europe and Australia

Non-Western Areas

Total World

1% 2% 3% 4% 5% 6% 7% 8% 9% 10%

better. About 70 percent of its membership lives in the Christian countries of the world, but still 70 percent of all the world population does not live there.

The optimist sees a 1 to 2 percent increase in the proportion of Christians to a total world population in the next decade. The pessimist expects that by the end of the 1970's the percentage of Christians in the world will be hardly 15 percent. For supporting evidence he points to the influence of urbanization and the technological revolution, the powerful mission activities of Islam and Buddhism, the rise of hundreds of new religions, and the continuous and rapid process of secularization within the Christian church—particularly in the West.

An example from Africa may illustrate more clearly the immensity of the unfinished task and its challenge to the church in the seventies. Adventists officially have a mission station in the Sudan, a country of over fifteen million people, but there are only three Seventh-day Adventists. That is one Adventist to every five million people. With a birthrate of 5.2 percent and a death rate of 2 percent, the population of the Sudan is expected to increase to twenty-two million during the seventies. Consequently, even if the Adventist population there increased 500 percent in the next ten years, the number of those not reached with the gospel would be larger at the end of the decade than at the beginning. The same holds true for Asia, where, although the Christian church grows 5 to 7 percent in many areas, the present population of two billion will probably double within twenty years.

A word of warning, however, is in place here. We cannot measure or express in numbers the kingdom of God. These serve only to describe an issue more concretely. Moreover, in practically all mission territories the number of those who claim to be Seventh-day Adventists far exceeds membership records. Population censuses in Africa and Latin America give membership figures that are often twice or three times as high as the figures on the church's own records. Nevertheless, the immensity of the task stands out very clearly.

Now, add to all this the inadequacy of financial resources in the non-Western areas of the world, the percentage decrease of mission offerings, the increased local spending by Western churches, and the lack of missionary enthusiasm, and a picture of a severe crisis emerges. Yet never before has there been a more urgent hour. Never before were the fields more ripe for harvesting or the opportunities greater for participating in Christ's own mission of reconciliation.

The Implications of the Situation

In the seventies the Adventist Church will feel very strongly the implications of these three prominent features. Some will be administrative and organizational in nature, such as the matter of proportionate representation of the overseas churches in the highest executive and policy-making body of the church. Another question will concern the priorities for spending funds on evangelism, on the community service branches of the church—education, medicine, welfare, and technical assistance—and on the care and administration of the members.

Other questions will arise over the proper distribution of finances. For example: Should Adventists spend their money largely in fields ripe for harvesting—areas such as the Central African Union, South Brazil, the Philippines, and Indonesia, where thousands of people wait to be led into the church—or should they spend it more evenly and continue to sow even on stony ground? Ample evidence from the history of mission indicates that as a result of the principle of equal distribution, tremendous harvests of souls could not be reaped because the money and personnel were used to support institutions or programs in areas where the Holy Spirit clearly had not yet prepared the field, let alone the harvest.

But questions like these can be answered only in the light of what mission really is, how the Spirit is leading, and what the nature and task of the church is in the world. The answers not only require a bold and honest look at what has been accomplished so far and what the position of the church is in the world today, but also they stress the need for a clear theology of mission. Without such a theology a missionary movement is directionless. The choices and decisions that have to be made and the church policies and priorities that must be determined all imply certain assumptions about the task and essence of mission. Acting without realizing the theological issues involved means following nontheological p r i n c i p l e s which often express only worldly motives.

A theology of mission is also badly needed for a proper evaluation of the success or failure in mission and for development of correct strategies and methods. "The varying circumstances taking place in our world," Ellen G. White wrote, "call for labor which will meet these peculiar developments." [3] In the light of many new developments it is not at all improbable that certain missionary institutions, policies, methods, and priorities of the past may have to be revised or even abandoned altogether—not because they were wrong, but simply because they have fulfilled their particular function.

New ways and new priorities may have to be developed which may even be contrary to what Adventists have usually considered good mission strategy or even "present truth." Ellen G. White warned, therefore, never to say, "This has never been taught." "Away with these restrictions. . . . That which God gives His servants to speak today would not perhaps have been present truth twenty years ago, but it is God's message for this time." [4] And, "Present truth, from the first letter of its alphabet to the last, means missionary effort." [5]

So let us look in more detail at a few aspects of the present missionary situation and their implications for the seventies.

The Front Lines

In the beginning of the Seventh-day Adventist missionary outreach, all overseas missionaries c a m e f r o m North America. They went to preach the Advent Message and to plant churches. And though this work is far from accomplished, Adventist churches are now firmly established over the whole globe. Not only is the Adventist Church the most widespread of all Protestant denominations, with the largest number of missionaries in the field, but in many areas of the world, particularly in Latin America, it is also the largest and fastest-growing single Protestant denomination.

In many non-Western areas the ratio of Adventists to non-Adventists already greatly exceeds that in Europe or the United States. In North America there is about one Adventist to over five hundred non-Adventists.[6] But in the Philippines the ratio is one to three hundred. In the Central African Union, one to sixty-five. Compare these ratios with those of Great Britain, one to five thousand. The Netherlands Union, one to four thousand. Or the Central European Division, one to two thousand. The questions naturally arise, then, What really constitutes a mission field? What is a missionary?

The church's present Western overseas missionary endeavor is characterized by Adventist workers leaving the largely non-Adventist areas of the West to work among large concentrations of Adventist believers overseas. These missionaries do not go out to work for nonbelievers in particular. Rather, they are employed by the church to work within the church, especially for the members of the church. The nature of the typical Adventist missionary's work indicates the same trend. Most Adventist overseas missionaries go out as teachers in Adventist *schools* (which usually admit only a few non-Adventist students), as medical personnel to work in Adventist *hospitals* (which are left as soon as a government takes over the institution), and a small percentage as *administrators*. Hardly any Adventist missionaries leave the shores of North America to proclaim Seventh-day Adventism to nonbelievers and to raise up churches. The church's Western overseas movement has largely developed into an *intrachurch movement*.

All too frequently the Christian considers that the front lines of mission, the boundaries one has to cross in order to be called a missionary, are *salt water* (the deeper and wider the ocean and the farther one travels from home, the more one is considered a missionary), and the barriers of *language* (if one learns the foreign language at all), of *culture* (if, indeed, one crosses this boundary), and of *geography* (climate and physical milieu).

In the Bible, however, the only real front line that makes a person a missionary is the boundary between belief and unbelief, between those who are "foreigners to God" and those who belong to "the household of God." Jesus never left Palestine. He never crossed salt water. He never learned a foreign language or lived with people whose strange customs He did not understand. Yet Ellen G. White rightly called Him "the greatest missionary the world has ever known." [7]

Christian mission is the imitation and the continuation of Christ's work on earth. Therefore, the only boundary that should determine mission for the church today is the boundary between belief and unbelief, which runs through every nation, tribe, and tongue. The front line of mission exists wherever people do not know Christ.

Such an understanding of mission boundaries ought to determine the church's priorities and help shape its future policies and organization. This is most imperative, since much of the church's missionary structure and organization reflect a concept of the world and of mission that is no longer capable of solving the problems and issues of the new missionary situation. Thus, many opportunities and challenges of mission go unanswered.

When the Adventist Church was by and large a North American church and when geographical expansion determined the essence of a missionary and his success, it was only natural for the church organization to reflect that situation. As a result, the world of Seventh-day Adventists became structurally divided into "home base" and "overseas divisions," which were often shaped according to the well-known geopolitical principles so characteristic of that day. And, although a few overseas fields have now been designated as home bases themselves, little has changed in the Adventist conceptualization and organization of mission in terms of geography, economy, and geopolitical principles. The General Conference has remained structurally an integral part of North America, which continues to be thought of as the center of Seventh-day Adventism's worldwide work and the home base for the whole world.

The priorities in spending denominational money also reflect this same attitude. As a result, for instance, the development and training of an Asian and African missionary force, probably the greatest need in Adventist mission today, receive hardly any financial attention.

Yet, success in mission during the next few decades will depend to a large degree on the successful recruitment and preparation of an African, Asian, and Latin American force of workers and leaders. Now that the era of Europe is over and the era of Asia has begun, an Asian and African missionary force ready to go to their own people will be the greatest asset of Seventh-day Adventist mission within the next decade.

In the same way, it is unfortunate that Adventists often continue to define the opportunities for mission according to the accessibility of an area to American missionaries. And they often spend funds accordingly. The unsatisfactory division of the African continent into four separate areas—Northern Europe-West Africa, Euro-Africa, Afro-Mideast, and Trans-Africa—is an issue at every General Conference session. Yet the solution to this problem, as to so many others, hinges on rethinking the boundaries and characteristics of mission.

A Two-way Street

With the rapid growth and solid establishment of the church overseas, the Adventist missionary movement is no longer a one-way street. At the moment almost as many missionaries are sent from overseas areas as from North America. This situation calls for some revision of Adventist mission policies, which were made when all missionaries came from North America and Europe. The Adventist Church in the Philippines alone has sent more missionaries overseas in the past few years than the Central European Division has. They now serve all over Asia and Africa. In the seventies this missionary movement from the non-Western church into all the world will greatly increase. (See Figure 3.)

When Adventist travel was a one-way street, the only link between the overseas field and North America was the missionary. His life and work became the standard by which the new overseas congregations judged the church and the country of the missionary's origin. In general, the congregations in the West had the excellent reputation of being self-sacrificing communities, burning with missionary zeal, living perfect and sanctified lives out of faith in the soon-coming Lord.

Mission: Possible

FIGURE 3
New Missionaries Sent (World Field, 1918 to 1968)

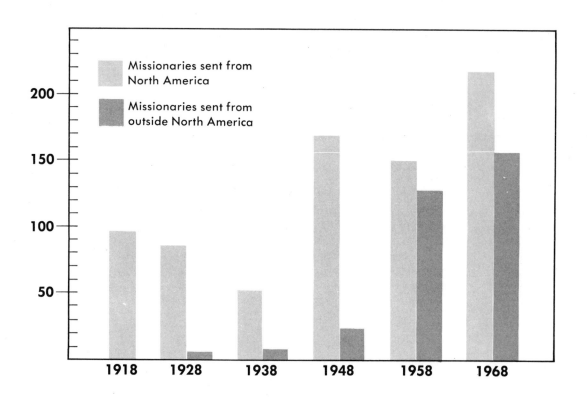

Today, h o w e v e r , Adventist travel is a two-way street, with workers from overseas divisions frequently coming to the United States. Some come to attend General Conference meetings. Many others, often the younger ones, come to study at Adventist c o l l e g e s and universities. What kind of church do they find? The impressions these people take home to their own churches often carry a very heavy weight for the present Adventist mission situation.

Furthermore, former mission fields have now been discovered to be prime tourist attractions. Hundreds of Adventists from North America, young and not so young, are visiting these remote beauty spots of the world. But the new mission-minded churches overseas judge visiting Adventists not as tourists but as representatives of the Adventist Church in North America. What image do these individuals or tourist groups leave behind? Is it the picture of a self-sacrificing, sanctified body of Christ? Every local church from Maine to Mississippi is now involved in determining the success or failure in their church's worldwide missionary outreach.

This whole new situation happened so suddenly and rapidly that it has caught the church by surprise. But then the ways of God's mission always come as a surprise. It is high time, however, for the church to wake up. Textbooks in church schools and mission reports in church magazines and Sabbath Schools still portray the thatched huts of cannibals, when, in reality, the people overseas are usually well-educated Adventists sitting in the same schools and audiences where these reports are being given.

Growth and Institutions

The fact that the Adventist overseas missionary movement has developed into an *intrachurch movement*, in the sense that the church spends most of the funds, time, and personnel for the church, is both the church's greatest strength and greatest weakness. Of a total Seventh-day Adventist working force of some seventy thousand people, roughly 40 percent work in Adventist schools for Adventist children, 30 percent in medical work, and 13 percent in administrative positions. Only 10 percent are engaged in pastoral work, and only a small percentage of these are doing evangelism. Adventists have invested over a billion dollars in buildings and equipment, of which barely 4 percent has been in publishing houses, Adventist Book Centers, and radio and television evangelism. Forty percent of this billion dollars has been invested in church buildings and educational institutions. Over $405 million has been invested in conferences and conference associations. (See Figures 4 and 5.)

Every year more than 40 percent of the total General Conference budget goes toward capital investment. This truly is a s t r e n g t h of the Adventist Church, which does far better than any other missionary organization in taking care of its members and in providing a Christian education for its children. And even though it loses through apostasy about thirty-five people for every one hundred who come into the church, this rate is rather low compared with that of other denominations. But unless the church keeps the proper perspective, its greatest strength may develop into its greatest weakness.

An increasing percentage of new members in overseas fields will come from Adventist families. Reliable statistics are not available, but it is estimated that in many areas of North America between 70 and 75 percent of all baptisms involve the church's own youth. In the Philippines, still a relatively young church, the percentage of new members from Adventist families is already about 60 percent.

Unless Seventh-day Adventism reconsiders its priorities, its membership expansion in the 1970's will more and more result from *biological growth*. Once again, this is a strong point, for Adventists are absolutely right in considering their own children and youth their first mission field. But the Master also wants the church to go out into the world to take the message of salvation and warning to those who do not know Christ. Therefore, the church should also aim at *conversion growth*, that is, leading non-Christians i n t o the "household of God."

The Seventh-day Adventist Church should honestly reevaluate its present policies to determine the priorities for expenditures and for personnel. Of the some 29,500 active Adventist workers in North America, 40 percent are employed in medical institutions, another 36

FIGURE 4
Percentage Distribution of Denominational Investments, 1970

Total Investment $1,311,417,548.58

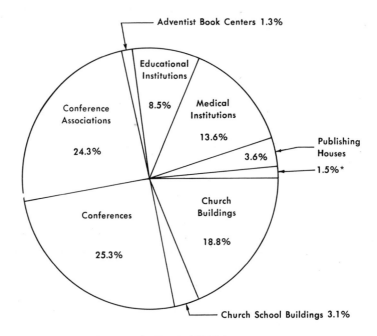

Adventist Book Centers 1.3%

Educational Institutions

8.5%

Conference Associations

24.3%

Medical Institutions

13.6%

3.6%

Publishing Houses

1.5%*

Church Buildings

18.8%

Conferences

25.3%

Church School Buildings 3.1%

OUTSIDE NORTH AMERICA

*1.5% (Includes: Industries, Radio/TV Evangelism, Temperance Societies, Servicemen's Centers)

$304,093,936.35, 23.2% of total denominational investment

FIGURE 4
(cont.)

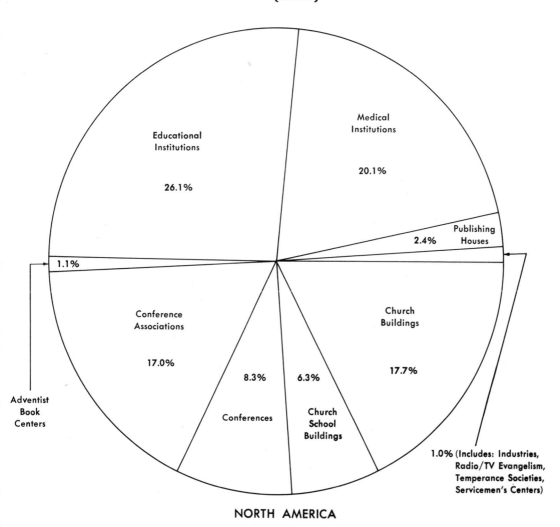

Educational
Institutions

26.1%

Medical
Institutions

20.1%

Publishing
Houses

2.4%

1.1%

Conference
Associations

17.0%

Church
Buildings

17.7%

8.3%

6.3%

Conferences

Church
School
Buildings

Adventist
Book
Centers

1.0% (Includes: Industries,
Radio/TV Evangelism,
Temperance Societies,
Servicemen's Centers)

NORTH AMERICA

$1,007,323,612.23, 76.8% of total denominational investment

FIGURE 5
Percentage Distribution of Denominational Investments, 1970
(Total World Field)

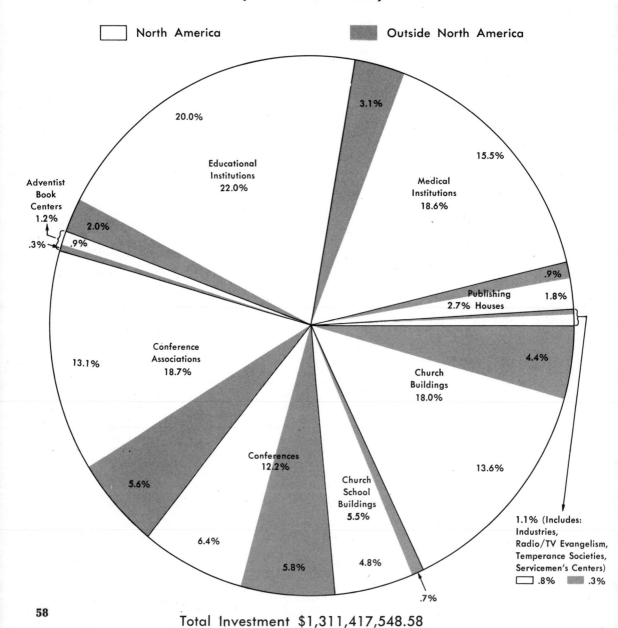

Total Investment $1,311,417,548.58

percent in education, and barely 8 percent in pastoral and evangelistic work. In this respect the Australasian Division shows a much healthier picture: some 19 percent involved in pastoral work and evangelism, 14 percent in medical work, and 25 percent in education.

If institutions absorb too much of a movement's money and personnel, stagnation results. We call it *institutionalism*. The expensive multiplication of colleges and universities, their concentration in a very small area of the world field, that is, in North America, the duplication of programs, the administrative overhead, the strong emphasis on big hospital work—all these tend to hinder the church's missionary outreach. The aim of institutions is to promote the *worldwide* missionary movement. But, at present, institutionalism is causing stagnation. In fact, in many areas it could prevent an increasing growth rate of the church in the seventies.

Determining the Priorities

In Europe and North America, 25 to 30 percent of the population is under fifteen years of age.

In the non-Western world, 45 to 50 percent is under fifteen, and 60 to 65 percent under twenty-five. The church explosion in various countries has, of course, resulted in a larger percentage of young people within the church. To accommodate them it would be necessary for the church to build five times as many schools in the next ten years in Latin America and Africa alone as it has built in all the world during the past hundred years.

The same figures, or even higher, apply to the need for teachers. The two Latin American divisions, with twice as many Adventist young people as the North American Division, have half as many academies and only a fourth the number of teachers as in North America. The picture of the concentration of college programs looks even worse.[8] The North American Division employs six times as many college teachers as do both Latin American divisions. And the whole African continent does not have even one fully accredited senior college!

Of all college and academy teachers in the denomination, over 60 percent are employed in North America—for less than 10 percent of all Adventist young people. Here lies, indeed, the church's greatest and most immediate need: a rapid expansion of education facilities and personnel to those areas of tremendous church growth. Here also lies the greatest challenge for North American college graduates in the seventies: voluntary teaching in Latin America, Asia, and Africa for a year or two. The Student Missionary Program is filling some of this need, but barely one percent of what is required.

Already thousands and thousands of non-Western Adventist children must attend non-Adventist schools at an age when they are most receptive to truth and falsehood. There simply are not enough local funds to support Adventist education, for *the church explosion is taking place in the poverty areas of the world.* Parents in these countries cannot afford to pay the high tuition of a private school, even if there were schools. Funds for very many new school buildings are just not available, even if the General Conference could double its appropriations to these overseas divisions.

Besides, North American Adventists, who supply most of the funds, are struggling themselves

to keep their schools open. But in South America and Africa the situation is so desperate that some 70 percent of their Adventist young people attend government schools. With most of the people in the world and in the church soon to be in the under-twenty-five category, the church must give immediate consideration to these youth in their various age groups and explore the possibilities and means of reaching and keeping them.

In the interim, the church might approach this problem in a threefold way by (1) emphasizing the *parents'* responsibility toward their own youth and revitalizing the religious-educational function of the family, (2) strengthening the *local church* programs for youth, especially for the 18 to 25 age group, and (3) rallying a corps of *youth volunteers* from North America and Europe to teach in Adventist schools overseas.

With the establishment of a larger A d v e n t i s t Voluntary Teacher Service Corps, people holding master's or bachelor's degrees could voluntarily, or for a very small salary, teach for a year or two in academies or elementary schools in Asia, Africa, and Latin America. If this cannot be done—and why can't it?—then the church explosion of the 1960's may well be followed by a mass apostasy in the 1970's. It has happened before in recent mission history and is one of the main reasons why the Protestant missionary movement of the nineteenth and early twentieth centuries lost its thrust.

The World of Illiteracy

Another factor in the world-wide mission of the church is that some 40 percent of the world population is illiterate. And every year the total increases by twenty-five to thirty million. These people, to a large extent, lie beyond the reach of the Adventist Church, which has grown and is growing largely through its publishing work. In Asia and Africa whole countries exist with 70 percent, or even more, of the population illiterate. Add to these numbers the large group of semiliterates—people who have gone to a primitive "village-school" for three to six years and who, since then, have never read anything—and the challenge stands out very clearly.

A large number of these illiterates have never even heard the name of Christ. Furthermore, these people, after conversion, cannot feed upon the Word of God by meditation and prayerful study. We all know how difficult it is to remain a faithful Christian without that. In addition, the march of literacy has produced a rift between the youth who have gone to school and the older people who "became" illiterate.[9] In the African and Asian societies, where authority rests with the older people, this has caused untold hardships and divisions between parents and children, the older and the younger generation. The ability to read and write seems to shift the authority pattern. Teaching these older people to read and write would mean a giant step toward bridging the gap between parents and children. This is not an unimportant aspect of the "Elijah message"—turning the hearts of the children to the parents and vice versa. (Malachi 4: 5, 6.)

And here is where a new Seventh-day Adventist educational program ought to come in—*a d u l t education.* Governments are usually very happy for missions to embark upon adult-education and literacy-education programs. Very few financial investments are necessary to implement and conduct such programs, yet the potential for the advancement of the gospel is incalculable. However, such programs would require hundreds of volunteers to lead out overseas. Like the English language schools in Japan, Korea, Indonesia, and other areas of Southeast Asia, these literacy programs could become an opening wedge to thousands of people who are now virtually shut away from the gospel. Adventism's response to this need in the seventies may determine whether millions of people in Africa and Asia will be won for Christ, communism, or anti-Christ.

The Harvest Is Ripe

Should the field, then, determine church priorities? Yes! We must look on the mushrooming church explosion in Latin America, Africa, and certain parts of Asia as a result of the work of the Holy Spirit. Whole villages and tribes, often with thousands of people, suddenly become receptive to the Advent Message; and there will be much more of this in the seventies, as the prophets foretold would happen in the last days.

Seventh-day Adventists are not harvesting one fiftieth of those who are ready to accept their message in those areas, as is evident from the thousands of people who call themselves Adventists in the censuses of Latin American and African countries, yet who are not on Adventist membership rolls. It is evident further from the phenomenal growth of other little-institutionalized Christian denominations in areas where the Spirit has prepared the harvest. Of course, criticism may be in order for the lack of "institutional care" many of those brought into the fold of those churches receive.

For the seventies, Seventh-day Adventists ought more than ever before to keep their eyes open for people whom the Spirit has prepared to join them. They ought to make funds and personnel available to harvest the fields that are ripe for harvest *now*. This, indeed, will require much greater flexibility in missionary approach and a shift in priorities and policies. Adventists tend to exhibit too much of the "three-more - months - and - then - the - harvest" idea. The establishment of an International Harvest Fund may create some of the needed flexibility. Then as soon as somewhere in the world a people becomes extraordinarily receptive to the gospel—as happens continuously—these funds can be made available to reap the harvest. At the same time, a pool of experienced missionaries can be ready to go out as harvesters as soon as the call arises.

One of the grave possibilities threatening the Seventh-day Adventist Church in the seventies is that because of certain traditional patterns it may let the harvest-time go by in areas that are ripe now, while it spends its funds, personnel, and efforts in sowing or cultivating elsewhere. Those men who are already preparing workers and funds for mainland China in order to be ready when God opens the door indicate that there are Adventist leaders who are spiritually clear-sighted.

A Lay Church

One of the greatest contributions the rapidly expanding congregations in the non-Western world will make to the Adventist Church as a whole in the seventies may well be the *rediscovery of the church as a lay church.* This concept characterized the early Christian church. It also marked the early Advent Movement. And certain signs indicate that the rediscovery of this Biblical c o n c e p t of the church and its mission has already begun. The burgeoning church growth of the sixties did not result primarily from big evangelistic campaigns or from the work of well-trained ministers. It came about as a result of the work of lay members who have lived out their faith and given an account of it in the fields, in the factories, and in the villages.

The developing church in the non-Western world is a lay church after the New Testament fashion, for the laity win the converts. Also the laity establish new congregations, and it should form the l e a d e r s h i p of the church. However, a high rate of illiteracy still mars many of the exploding churches in the non-Western areas. Although the laity have produced the church growth, they are not yet educated to become its leader. Right now, therefore, Adventism must accommodate itself to the increasing number of new members and churches by multiplying institutes for lay church leaders—institutes that will prepare those who have produced the growth to become its leaders.

If the Holy Spirit can use these often-uneducated members of the church to win thousands of converts, it is only a small thing for the church to give them extra training and to entrust them with leadership. Why not *ordain* such individuals as well, even though the church does not employ them as such? If the Holy Spirit has ordained them to be co-workers with Christ, what right does the church have to withhold its official recognition? [10]

Right now, in some areas, lay institutes have far greater priority than the establishment of a theological seminary, however important that may be, in Asia, Latin America, or Africa. For the time being, such seminaries could be organized in the form of extension schools. A special committee should start working out the details of a greatly expanded system of seminary and university *extension schools* in all the world. Such a program would solve the immediate problem of p r o v i d i n g sufficient church personnel and lay workers.

Lay Missionaries

Another aspect of a lay church is its lay missionaries. The success of a missionary movement is proportionally related to its ability to rally the whole church, that is, all its members, to the task of mission. Ellen G. White never grew tired of reiterating this truth: "All who receive the life of Christ are ordained to work for the salvation of their fellow-men." "All are alike called to be missionaries for God." [11]

Because Adventists have failed to enlist all their members in mission, the work has remained unfinished. "If those who claimed to have a living experience in the things of God had done their appointed work as the Lord ordained, the whole world would have been warned ere this, and the Lord Jesus would have come in power and great glory." [12]

Two primary reasons exist, then, for developing a lay mission program—one theological and one practical.

Theologically speaking, Christ entrusted His work of reconciliation to the laity as a whole. When He said, "Go ye into all the world," that "ye" meant *all* who believe on His name. To prepare the people for their task of mission, God has given them special gifts: apostles, preachers, supervisors, teachers, etc. (Ephesians 4:7, 11-16.) The main responsibility of these special ministries is to nourish, equip, help, and sustain the community of believers in carrying out its mission. In other words, God has called the ministers and leaders to assist His people in carrying out the mission of the church, not vice versa, as is often the case.

"In laboring where there are already some in the faith, the minister should *at first* seek not so much to convert believers, as to train the church-members . . . to work for others." [13] In the New Testament church, authority rested on a man's ministry and the word he preached, not on his position. Success or failure in the work of God depends on the way in which the church prepares and rallies its whole membership to mission.

Practically speaking, *the possibilities of lay witness constitute the church's greatest opportunity to penetrate into the whole world with the gospel in the seventies.* In many areas of the world and many spheres of life, the minister cannot work or is no longer listened to. The Sudan, with its three Adventists in a population of some fifteen million, does not allow foreign missionaries to en-

ter. Yet at the same time the university at Khartoum is crying for staff members, and the government desperately wants doctors, engineers, and teachers.

Senegal shows a similar picture, and so do hundreds of other areas. The governments in many places where the church cannot get official permission to enter or to expand its missionary work are seeking specialists of all sorts. The future of Adventist mission work in the People's Republic of China may well be determined by this concept of lay missionaries: businessmen, engineers, journalists, etc., who will go there and through their excellent performance and holy life make Seventh-day Adventism known to the millions who see and hear them.

The greatest opportunities for mission work in the seventies will include Adventist engineers working for the Arabian Oil Company, Adventist secretaries going overseas for companies in areas where the church is weak, and Adventist teachers, doctors, and technicians applying for jobs with governments in Africa, Asia, and Latin America. In 1970 alone, some 26,000 job openings were listed in these areas. Of course, the same principle applies at home in places where ministers often cannot find a hearing—the universities, industry, and mass communications. We often hear that the church should go into such areas, but the church is already there in the person of its laity.

Ellen G. White warned the church that its members should not congregate in large concentrations but should live scattered in small companies[14] as was the pattern of the early Christian church. Who could forecast how the church might grow in the seventies if Seventh-day Adventists spread themselves out and began a concerted lay mission effort—some moving to the needy rural or thickly populated areas of the United States and others going into the world field to make their application of Christian witness in whatever job they chose?

To put all this into practice and make the Adventist lay witness operation most effective, the General Conference could establish an office called Advent-

ists A b r o a d—an organization that would inform Adventist businessmen, professors, technicians, doctors, engineers, and others of the specific opportunities for service in such areas as Africa and Asia, and then help them contact the appropriate recruiting services in order to apply for these positions. Before these people would leave on their overseas assignment, the agency could offer a short, high-powered training and orientation institute, at the church's expense, in Christian witness. Continual communication between these laymen and the agency in the form of letters and visits from church leaders would promote mission as soon as they were overseas.

Christ organized the church for a missionary purpose, and He desires to see the whole church devising ways and means whereby rich and poor, black and white, free and bond, may hear the message of truth.[15] With vision, faith, and power in the church, God's mission may be finished in the seventies.

[1] Unless notation is made otherwise, statistics have been taken from annual church reports.

[2] Ellen G. White, Fundamentals of Christian Education (Nashville, Tennessee: Southern Publishing Association, 1923), p. 293.

[3] Ellen G. White, Manuscript 8a, 1888, as printed in A. V. Olson, Through Crisis to Victory, 1888-1901, p. 273.

[4] Ibid., pp. 273, 274.

[5] Ellen G. White, Counsels on Health, p. 300.

[6] It should be kept in mind that chil-

dren are not included in the number of Adventists reported.

[7] Ellen G. White, *Welfare Ministry* (Washington, D.C.: Review and Herald Publishing Association, 1952), p. 118; see also, Ellen G. White, *Medical Ministry* (Mountain View, California: Pacific Press Publishing Association, 1932), p. 15.

[8] A question the church should study is whether it is wise to continue to spend so much of its money on its colleges and universities. According to N. R. Dower, "Europe—Land of Promise," *Review and Herald,* January 1, 1970, p. 16, 70 to 80 percent of Adventist youth in the Central European Division stay in the church even though no Adventist schools are there. That percentage is barely reached in North America, where the church is better equipped with schools than in any other area in the world. Apparently the retention of youth in the church may depend much less on having Adventist schools, particularly colleges and universities, than has been assumed.

[9] Illiteracy is defined in contrast to literacy. Before literacy penetrated these parts of the world, the people were not illiterate; they were, by definition, non-literate.

[10] "The ceremony of the laying on of hands added no new grace or virtual qualification. It was an acknowledged form of designation to an appointed office, and a recognition of one's authority in that office. *By it the seal of the church was set upon the work of God.*"—Ellen G. White, *The Acts of the Apostles* (Mountain View, California: Pacific Press Publishing Association, 1911), pp. 161, 162. (Italics supplied.)

[11] Ellen G. White, *The Desire of Ages,* p. 822; Ellen G. White, *The Ministry of Healing* (Mountain View, California: Pacific Press Publishing Association, 1909), p. 395.

[12] Ellen G. White, "Whosoever Will, Let Him Come," *Advent Review and Sabbath Herald,* October 6, 1896, p. 629.

[13] Ellen G. White, *Gospel Workers* (revised and enlarged edition; Washington, D.C.: Review and Herald Publishing Association, 1936), p. 196. (Italics supplied.)

[14] See, for example, Ellen G. White, *Instruction for Effective Christian Service* (Washington, D.C.: Review and Herald Publishing Association, 1947), p. 178.

[15] Ellen G. White, *Testimonies to Ministers and Gospel Workers,* p. 204; White, *The Acts of the Apostles,* pp. 9-16.

Christ's Mission and Ours

Christ established His church for a missionary purpose. Its whole life and liturgy, work and worship, therefore, has a missionary intention if not a missionary dimension. Mission is the church's very *raison d'être*. God has claimed for His own the members of the church—the people whom God, through His Holy Spirit, has called out of darkness into His marvelous light—to proclaim His glory. (1 Peter 2:9.) "All who receive the life of Christ are ordained to work for the salvation of their fellowmen. For this work the church was established, and all who take upon themselves its sacred vows are thereby pledged to be co-workers with Christ." [1]

The church's mission, then, is to participate in God's own mission. Itself the fruit of God's mission of love, the church is His agency for the salvation of men, an instrument to carry the gospel into all the world and to gather people from every nation into the one household of God. The church, as a living image of God, must reflect His fullness and sufficiency through unselfish love, service, and a holy way of life. [2]

A Solution to Sin

God's mission is His way of dealing with the problem of sin and its destructive power. Before sin entered the world, a rebellion had arisen in heaven against God's government. In opposition to God's kingdom, its laws and its principles, Satan established a kingdom of his own. (Revelation 12:7-9.) He also deceived our first p a r e n t s—in whose fall all men die (1 Corinthians 15:22)—and he continues to move men to disobey God (Genesis 3; Ephesians 6:11; 1 Peter 5:8). Nothing in creation is protected from his evil power. Sin and suffering, decay and death, result. But God, who does not want any man to suffer or to perish (Ezekiel 18:23; John 3:16, 17; 2 Peter 3:9), has sent His angels and His Spirit to protect men and to guide them. He sends help and redemption. (Psalms 20: 2; 111:9.) He sends men to bless others and His prophets to make Himself known as He really is. Our God is a missionary God, who so loves the world that He sent His only Son to restore the broken relationships and to establish His peace. The church is both a sign and an instrument of God's sending activity.

Restoration the Goal

The goal of God's mission, in which the church is called to participate, is restoration of His kingdom. The devil and his rule will be destroyed, and sin and death abolished. The forces of evil that separate man from his Creator and which "dehumanize" him will be overthrown. God will re-create man in His own image, and of his own free will man will love and honor Him. The principles and laws of God's kingdom will stand vindicated, and the whole universe will "be freed from the shackles of mortality and enter upon the liberty and splendour of the children of God." (Romans 8:21.)

This goal of God's mission—the restoration of His kingdom—can hardly be overemphasized. To that very end God sent Jesus, whose life and mission form the model of all mission. For that very purpose Christ also called the church into existence. Each function, each institution, and each activity of the church has meaning—and a right to exist—only as it leads to that goal. No church, therefore, must set up goals that center in itself, its members, or its doctrines. God's great goal and the church's role as His servant forbid an ecclesiocentric approach to mission.

Neither should the church seek its goals in mere social action: freeing the world from hunger, disease, poverty, social injustice, and the establishing of a Christian culture. The kingdom of God is not identical with "a better world." Moreover, sin constantly turns men into rebels. On the other hand, the Christian church cannot find its goals merely in the rescuing of individual souls and the planting of churches. Surely, God's mission is always to seek and to save what is lost (Luke 19:10), but the kingdom of God is not identical with the sum of converts. It embraces much more than individual acts of salvation. After all, mission centers in God, not in man.[3]

Both goals—the rescuing of men from sin and the fight against disease, hunger, social injustice, and the evil structures of society—are aspects of the conflict raging between Christ and Satan and, therefore, are truly a sign and a part of God's mission activity. But much more is at stake. All these different goals must be viewed in that wider cosmic perspective of the full restoration of God's kingdom. "Set your mind on God's kingdom and his justice before everything else, and all the rest will come to you as well." (Matthew 6:33.)

The Kingdom Established

God accomplished His mission in the sending of His Son, Jesus Christ. Through His life and death, Christ established God's kingdom.[4] The whole New Testament message pivots around "The kingdom has come." During His earthly ministry, Christ unmasked Satan and revealed his character as that of a liar and a murderer. (John 8:44.) God sent His Son to destroy the works of the devil, and He indeed defeated him. (Luke 10:18.) Christ's suffering and death revealed the true nature of sin. At the same time, they also revealed the true character of God and the foundation of His kingdom: love, freedom, justice, and obedience. Christ has restored man's relationships with God and with his fellows. Christ has called His church to serve as living evidence of the ensuing peace, that new relationship of peace and reconciliation, of wholeness, well-being, and righteousness. (Romans 14:7; 2 Corinthians 5:19.)

Christ has, in fact, brought an end to sin and has broken its power, even the power of death.

He has expiated iniquity and taken away man's guilt. (John 1:29; Romans 8:3. Cf. Isaiah 53; Daniel 9:24.) The accuser of the brothers is overthrown. Now is the hour of victory for our God, the hour of His sovereignty and power. (Revelation 12:7-10.) For the church nothing is left to be done but *to make these events known* in all the world through proclamation, service, and fellowship and *to urge* the people for whom Christ died—Hindus and Buddhists, Muslims and the men of primitive faith, those born into Christian families, secularists and Communists—*to accept* this gospel and *to avail* themselves of its benefits.

Such mission calls for a decision, which involves being baptized and taking a place in God's church. Unless, then, we are "hawking the word of God about," mission will become to some "a vital fragrance" and to others "a deadly fume that kills." (2 Corinthians 2:15-17; Romans 1:16-24.) No one whom the Lord has drawn to His marvelous light is exempt from participating in this mission either as career-missionaries, as tent-making missionaries, or as nonprofessional missionaries, who are the greatest asset of God's church in the world today. God's love leaves us no choice. (2 Corinthians 5:14.) When the good news of the kingdom has been preached in all the world, then the end will come. (Matthew 24:14.) Mission, therefore, always means preparing for the return of Christ and the full realization of His kingdom.

The Whole World

In His sending activity, God always aims at the whole world. The church's mission, therefore, stands and falls with the understanding that God loves the whole world and that He has chosen the church as a channel of His grace to all men. Therefore, if God elects certain people and sends them special revelations of His glory, special truths, or blessings in any other form, it is always an *election for service*.

The history of God's mission on earth, however, is full of human misappropriations which have hindered the restoration of God's kingdom. Israel failed on this point by cherishing "the idea that they were the favorites of heaven, and that they were always to be exalted as the church of God." [5] Instead of mingling with all the people on earth, they "shut themselves away from the world as a safeguard against being seduced into idolatry." [6]

God then called another people into existence, likewise a holy nation and a royal priesthood, to proclaim the triumphs of Him who has called them out of darkness into His marvelous light. (1 Peter 2:9, 10.) "That which God purposed to do for the world through Israel, . . . He will finally accomplish through His church on earth today." [7] Christians would do well to remember, however, that all those things which happened in the past have been recorded for their instruction and warning. (Romans 15:4; 1 Corinthians 10: 11.) The danger of the church following in the footsteps of Israel of old is very real today. "The spirit which built up the partition wall between Jew and Gentile is still active." [8]

Christ calls the church "the salt of the earth." (Matthew 5: 13.) It can fulfill this function only when its members become scattered all over the world, mingle with its people, become involved in their activities, and thereby season and save the world. This does not mean that the church should become like the world, as many maintain, for "if the salt becomes tasteless, . . . it is . . . good for nothing." It does mean that God's mission is always accomplished through incarnation. No program, institution, or communications-satellite will do much good unless the world sees the gospel of Christ exemplified through His own people in their daily lives—in the way they have solved the daily problems of self and society, in their service to their fellowmen, and in the genuine Christian fellowship of the community of faith.

Neither is the church's mission fulfilled when it has merely crossed geographical boundaries. The world is a colorful mosaic of diverse groupings: sociological, economical, political, cultural, linguistic, religious, consanguineal, racial, and geographical. And the church must cross each frontier, of whatever kind, in fulfilling its missionary task. The church must present the gospel to men in the actual situation they live in, remembering that the situations keep changing.

An Uncompleted Mission

Christ's mission did not end at the cross, however. The very fact that Christ sent His followers into all the world *after* His resurrection to make the good news known, and only then, shows that the kingdom of God has not yet completely been realized. And the sending of the Holy Spirit after Christ's ascension testifies to the same.

Some have concluded, therefore, that Jesus failed in His mission, but they misunderstand the gospel. The kingdom has come. Christ has accomplished God's mission. (John 17:4; 19:30.) Others have reasoned that the kingdom indeed came, but that it now has to be realized in the hearts and the activities of all men. The mission of the church, in their opinion, involves the expansion of the kingdom that Christ established, like a little seed that grows into a full tree. Another group holds that world mission started after Christ's death as a reaction on the part of a disappointed group of Jewish followers of Jesus. They claim that the Christian mission, and the whole church that is the result of it, began as a crisis movement.

The debate continues in a rather heated way. Over against those who hold that the kingdom of God has already been fully realized in Christ and at Pentecost, stand those who maintain that it is all still future. One school of thought sees Christian mission as the very factor that will bring about the kingdom of God, while another considers mission itself as the evidence of that kingdom. Voices are heard that try to demythologize mission, and many believe that mission should be abandoned altogether.

All these schools of thought reveal a tension inherent in the New Testament and in Jesus' teachings in particular. We cannot escape that tension. It is important, then, that we cling to the whole Christ and His entire work of mission. The Scriptures make it abundantly clear that Christ has come, once and for all establishing God's kingdom. But they teach us just as clearly that Christ, after His ascension, had to fulfill another part of His mission before He would return and bring about the complete realization of the kingdom when every kind of rival domination, authority, and power will be abolished. (1 Corinthians 15:12-27.)

An understanding of Christ's continuing mission in the interim between His ascension and His return is absolutely indispensable for the church to have a right concept of mission, for the church's mission is none other than to imitate and to participate in the whole mission of Jesus Christ. If based on the accomplished work of Christ alone, the church's mission loses its direction and is robbed of its urgency. In the past this has led to inertia in mission and has tended to "humanize" the activities of the church. On the other hand, Christian mission that focuses only on the future event lacks the historical foundations which guarantee that our hope and expectations will be fulfilled. Such mission often leads to fanaticism, unbiblical enthusiasm, and overstrained expectations, which leave the church in great despair.

Only when its mission rests on the accomplished work of Christ, finding its strength, vision, and guidance from Christ's own activity in heaven today, through His Holy Spirit, will the church be able to accomplish its task. Mission, then, becomes a continuous preparation for the second coming of Christ, without being shaken when the "immediate consummation" of the kingdom does not take place tomorrow. But we will "look eagerly for the coming of the Day of God and work to hasten it on." (2 Peter 3:12.)

Christ's activities in the "heavenly places," the very source and power of Christian mission, may be described under three headings:

1. Christ as Lord and Ruler of all things.
2. Christ as our Mediator and High Priest.
3. Christ as Judge of all.

Christ As Lord

Christ is Lord. (1 Corinthians 12:3; 8:5, 6; Philippians 2:9-11; Ephesians 1:19-23.) Full authority has been given to Him, and on the basis of that power, He sends us into all the world. (Matthew 28:18, 19.) Without Christ's Lordship there would be no mission of the church. The continuous execution of Christ's Lordship on the world, a focal point in contemporary theological discussion, should not be too narrowly defined.

On the one hand, it means Christ's rule over those who believe in Him. He lives in them and gives them power to remain conquerors. Christ stands up for His church and prepares the way for its mission. Political "curtains," social "barriers," and legislative "closed doors" would form insurmountable obstacles to mission if Christ our Lord were not our missionary-in-chief.[9] He still has a way of walking through closed doors, and by His word He calms the storms and the unruly waves. And where the church in its missionary outreach meets opposition, Christ continually opens up opportunities for effective work. (1 Corinthians 16:9.)

On the other hand, Christ's rule also extends to all the affairs of this world. He holds all history in His hand. Whether it be war, revolution, technological change, or economic power, Christ remains above them all—always in control. It testifies of a lack of faith and a misunderstanding of Christ's mission in heaven if we think that this world still has to be subject to other powers. In fact, only because of God's mercy, shown in His Lordship through mission, has He not yet made an end to these powers of the world. But the church's mission will irrevocably lead to that end.

The Book of Revelation gives a powerful description of Christ's activities in heaven. John sees all the power of Christ directed toward the great goal of mission—the restoration of God's kingdom. The church is called to participate in this great mission of Christ through obedience and faithful witness, humble service and love.

Christ As High Priest

When Christ ascended into heaven to be crowned Lord of lords and King of kings, He also entered to be anointed as the High Priest to appear in the presence of God *for us*. (Hebrews 4: 14; 9:24.) Stephen saw Christ standing there as the Son of man (Acts 7:56), and John saw Him as the Lamb (Revelation 5). All this teaches us again that there is no mission without incarnation and sacrifice, humiliation and suffering.

Christ's activity as High Priest is a work of reconciliation. It is true that Christ had accomplished His mission of reconciliation on earth by sacrificing Himself, but the uniqueness and finality of that sacrifice is not a finality without continuation, not a static uniqueness. Our great High Priest lives continually to make intercession. (Hebrews 7: 25.) Christ, who died at the cross for all men, continues to plead our cause. (Romans 8:17, 34; 1 John 2:1.) The Book of Hebrews emphatically points out that Christ offered Himself once and once only, but it states equally emphatically that Christ continues His ministry in heaven to complete His mission of reconciliation. This is a profoundly important matter for a Christian understanding of mission, based on a widely accepted doctrine of the Person of Christ.

A key to the understanding of Christ's mission of reconciliation after His ascension may be found in the Old Testament sacrificial system, the shadow and antitype of the heavenly reality. In the Old Testament, the shedding of blood made atonement. But the completion of the reconciliation between the sinner and God demanded something more than the mere killing of the sacrifice. Over and above the sacrifice it included the *application* of the atoning sacrifice and the *appropriation* of its benefits by faith. Taking the blood, therefore, to the "holy place" and sprinkling it on the altar, played an essential part of the ritual. The covenant had as its aim not merely the expiation of sin—accomplished by the killing of the sacrifice—but the reestablish-ment of a union between sinful man and God. A clear illustration of this twofold aspect of reconciliation is found in Deuteronomy 21:1-9, where a law is given concerning the expiation of an unknown murderer.

So it is with Christ's mission. The goal is not just the expiation of sins, but the full reconciliation between God and each individual sinner. At the cross Christ removed the obstacle of reconciliation. But it is equally necessary that Christ, after shedding His blood, bring it before God's throne to apply His atoning sacrifice.

Christ has enlisted us in His mission of reconciliation (2 Corinthians 5:18), first to proclaim to all the world the great event of the accomplished sacrifice by which the obstacle to man's reconciliation has been removed, and, second, but equally important, to urge people of all nations, cultures, tribes, and religions to come boldly before God's throne, where Christ, our High Priest, applies His sacrifice for us. (Hebrews 10:19-22.) The church's mission of reconciliation is, therefore, never completed just with proclamation. It must call for a decision on the part of the listener to appropriate by faith the benefits of Christ's work for himself. "Sharing in God's work, we urge this appeal upon you: you have received the grace of God; do not let it go for nothing." 2 Corinthians 6:1.

While we cannot fully explain the nature of Christ's priestly ministry, God has revealed enough for us to know for sure that Christ is our intercessor (Romans 8:34; Hebrews 7:25) and our advocate (1 John 2:1)— our mediator (1 Timothy 2:5). Surely Christ's intercessory work in man's behalf is just as essential to accomplish His mission of restoration and reconciliation as was His death upon the cross.[10] The church cannot neglect this aspect of its mission either.

Mission, then, always includes a call to repentance (Acts 2:37-39), to walk in the newness of life that comes as a result of man's at-one-ment with God, and to live a consecrated and sanctified life so that we can stand before our God and Father holy and faultless in Christ (1 Thessalonians 1:9, 10; 3:13; 4:16). This makes the teaching of patterns of behavior, discipline, and obedience to God's holy law an essential part of the church's mission. The church should present these patterns of behavior in such a way that others can accept them as a true and necessary response to the gospel of Christ. Discipline must be understood as the nurturing of discipleship and obedience to God's holy law as a fruit of the new relationship with God. Christ works in us so that we do not continue in sin. (1 John 4:9-21; 5:1-5.) [11]

Christ As Judge

Christ's mission in the heavenly sanctuary—and, through His church, His mission on earth —will not go on endlessly. "He must be received into heaven until the time of universal restoration comes, of which God spoke by his holy prophets." Acts 3:21. The church's mission will lead to the return of Christ, when He will completely restore God's kingdom. This is the third and last act of Christ in which the church is called to participate: the work of judgment.

The Scriptures do not present this work of judgment as some new or gloomy event isolated from Christ's other mission activities. Did not Christ Himself say that He was sent into the world for judgment? (John 9:

39.) The meaning of these words is clear. Christ came to restore sight to the blind, to feed the hungry, to liberate the prisoners, and to bring justice to the oppressed. With Him a whole new order came, an order which is not of this world.

But, of course, His laws and principles clash with the existing social order, where selfishness and lawlessness abound and where the rich and the proud are in control. These people view the restoration of the divine kingdom as a dreadful event. "He hath put down the mighty from their seats, . . . and the rich he hath sent empty away." Luke 1: 52, 53, K.J.V. Jesus said, "Now is the judgment of this world; now shall the prince of this world be cast out." John 12:31, K.J.V. And he was—at the cross.

Although the judgment began at the cross, it did not end there, as some believe. The hour of judgment when the discrimination between those who have the faith of Jesus and those who refuse to obey His word becomes final did not take place then. (Acts 24:24; 2 Corinthians 5:10; Hebrews 9:27; 2 Peter 2:4.) This final judgment is the direct consequence of Christ's incarnation, death, and resurrection.

By their response to the Light, the Way, and the Truth, men declare themselves and, thus, pronounce their own judgment. "The man who puts his faith in him does not come under the judgement; but the unbeliever has already been judged in that he has not given his allegiance to God's only Son." John 3:18, 19. Christian mission always leads to such a discriminating (krisis) between those who believe in Christ and keep His commandments and those who do not.

The church's mission does not end when it merely proclaims or announces. "In every discourse fervent appeals should be made to the people to forsake their sins and turn to Christ." [12] "For we must all appear before the judgment seat of Christ, that every one may receive the things done in his body, according to that he hath done, whether it be good or bad." 2 Corinthians 5: 10, K.J.V. (Cf. Romans 2:6; 1 Peter 1:17 ff.)

The closer we come to the end of time, the clearer this process of sifting will become. (Matthew 13:36-43.) The acceptance or the rejection of Christ's love will be final. However, missionary and theological literature

Christ's Mission and Ours

pays surprisingly little attention to this aspect of Christ's mission. And yet Scripture says a great deal about it. The final judgment is an essential and inalienable aspect of Christ's mission and one of the strongest incentives to Christian mission in these last days.

Both the Old and New Testaments refer to a special activity of judgment by our High Priest in heaven. The Book of Hebrews gives a rather detailed account of Christ's service, which culminates in the total cleansing and consecration of God's people. After that, when sin is done away with, "Christ . . . will appear a second time . . . to bring salvation to those who are watching for him." (Hebrews 9: 26-28.) Peter, in Acts 3:19-22, and the parables of Christ (Matthew 18:23-25; 22:1-14; etc.) attest to this activity of Christ just before He returns, namely, the "wiping out of sin" and the final discrimination b e t w e e n the righteous and sinners. In the ritual of the Day of Atonement another clear picture emerges of our High Priest's final work. (Leviticus 16.)

The prophet Daniel describes the final activities in heaven as a courtroom scene (Daniel 7:9, 10), and other prophets, such as Joel and Zechariah, describe the scenes in their own way. But this much is clear: There is an "hour of judgment" (Revelation 14:7), which brings the mission of Christ and of His church to an end. The sentence is made public—the prophet says the books were opened—to the myriads of beings. This means it is final. It cannot be changed.

"All who have truly repented of sin, and by faith claimed the blood of Christ as their atoning sacrifice, have had pardon entered against their names in the books of heaven; as they have become partakers of the righteousness of Christ, and their characters are found to be in harmony with the law of God, their sins will be blotted out, and they themselves will be accounted worthy of eternal life." [13] Those who rejected Christ will die in their sins, destroyed along with death and the devil.

The Final Phase

Time prophecy indicates that this final phase of Christ's mission has already begun. Now is the time when God's mission is being fulfilled. We live on borrowed time. Christ's mission through His church on earth prevents the walls of history from collapsing.

About the same time as Christ began the last phase of His work in the heavenly sanctuary, a missionary awakening on earth—unequaled since the beginning of the church—took hold of the Christian church. New missionary societies sprouted in every part of the Christian world. Thousands of missionaries left the shores of North America and Europe, reporting mass conversions from everywhere in the world. Such a vast and rapid missionary expansion is evidence that Christ Himself is the missionary-in-chief. Through His delegates on earth He is bringing His mission to an end.

Let us make no mistake here: The tremendous religious revival and evangelical awakening, the universal expectation of a soon-coming King, and the sudden rise of missionary societies—all of which characterized the first half of the nineteenth century—were not merely the result of socio-economic or psychological factors, as many would have us believe. They directly accompany Christ's work. All mission has its origin in Him who sends.

He moves people and works in them, inspiring both the will and the deed "for his own chosen purpose." (Philippians 2:13.) And that purpose is clear: To bring His mission to an end and to restore the kingdom.

The conviction that Christ had entered upon His last phase of mission, namely, to bring about the restoration of all things through His work of judgment, brought the Seventh-day Adventist Church into existence, now the most widespread single Protestant missionary movement in the world. Adventists believe that God has called them to participate in Christ's own mission to prepare the world for His imminent return. Their mission is to present the gospel in such a way, through a comprehensive mission approach, that every person on earth will see Christ as his Saviour, his Lord, and his Judge and prepare for His soon coming. This is far more than the teaching of a set of doctrines; it is a mission of restoration— the restoration of God's holy law and of every principle of God's kingdom,[14] the restoration of man in the image of God, the vindication of God's sovereignty, and the defeat of everything evil, rebellious, and unholy.

There is no room for trivialities here. This mission requires the church to cross every socio-geographic, cultural, political, and religious boundary. The Seventh-day Adventist Church does not insist that only through its own witness can Christ make Himself known, but it cannot leave to others the witness to which Christ has called it. Adventists "recognize every agency that lifts up Christ before men as a part of the divine plan for the evangelization of the world," [15] but they wish at the same time to bear their witness freely, openly, in the world.

In its mission the church must avoid both a wrongly conceived confessionalism and a wrongly conceived ecumenism. An ecumenism which seeks unity of witness without a clear statement of the Word of God as it must be proclaimed in the present situation invites confusion and further fragmentation. It leads the church to disobedience. On the other hand, a wrongly conceived confessionalism holds to a particular confession for no other than traditional, human, ecclesiological reasons. It refuses to be open to the always dynamic Word of God, the Christian's source of truth. The church of God stands in constant need of critical self-examination and an openness to God's Word and to the world in order to fulfill its mission.

[1] Ellen G. White, The Desire of Ages, p. 822.

[2] Ellen G. White, The Acts of the Apostles, p. 9.

[3] Ellen G. White, The Great Controversy, pp. 502-504.

[4] Ibid., p. 347.

[5] Ellen G. White, Christ's Object Lessons (Washington, D.C.: Review and Herald Publishing Association, 1941), p. 294.

[6] Ellen G. White, The Story of Prophets and Kings (Mountain View, California: Pacific Press Publishing Association, 1917), p. 708; see also, White, The Acts of the Apostles, p. 14.

[7] White, Prophets and Kings, pp. 713, 714; see also pp. 374, 375 and The Great Controversy, p. 451.

[8] White, The Desire of Ages, p. 403.

[9] Ellen G. White, Fundamentals of Christian Education, p. 293.

[10] White, Great Controversy, p. 489.

[11] Ellen G. White, "The Law Exalted by Christ," Advent Review and Sabbath Herald, May 23, 1899, pp. 321, 322.

[12] Ellen G. White, Gospel Workers (revised and enlarged edition), p. 159.

[13] White, The Great Controversy, p. 483.

[14] White, Prophets and Kings, pp. 677, 678.

[15] Constitution, Bylaws, and Working Policy of the General Conference of Seventh-day Adventists, revised edition, October, 1970, p. 185.

That Curious Word "Missionary"

A cursory glance at our daily newspapers and magazines will convince us of the confusing pluralism in the use of the term "mission." A few months ago headlines in a national newspaper proclaimed, "Uniformed White House Guards Protect Foreign Missions." That was the day after demonstrators had attacked a number of consulates and embassies of countries behind the Iron Curtain. The title struck me, for it seemed to epitomize the confusion that exists nowadays concerning the term "mission."

In one newspaper that day alone, I found many other uses of the term "mission": Apollo mission, peace mission, mission commander, B-52 mission, mission control, economic mission, U.N. mission, search-and-destroy mission, presidential mission, etc. In a letter to the editor, a lady asked the reading public to assist her in a mission to secure books for the local library, and a man let the editor know that he had embarked upon a "mission to clean the old Baptist mission from excrements of hundreds of pigeons whose mission it apparently is to defile the mission building."

The owner of a local restaurant advertised his special attraction for the next day in the words, "Do some missionary work at lunchtime," and even Snoopy, the famous dog in "Peanuts," felt a mission call that day. "My mission," Snoopy said in his own haughty way, "is to destroy their hope." *That* is gospel mission according to Peanuts. Being curious about the great variety of meanings of this word *mission,* I checked a dictionary and found: "assignment, c a l l i n g , deputation, vocation, charge, embassy, legation, mandate," plus ten more ways to use the word.

But it is not just outside the church, but inside as well, that the term "mission" is used so loosely that confusion reigns. In o u r ecclesiastical vocabulary "mission" means, first of all, any type of church work done outside of one's own country. Persons who in this country are called a physics teacher, a high school principal, or a builder are all of a sudden called "missionaries" when they c r o s s salt water or a national boundary. The term "missionary" is here used over against the "national worker," and the "mission quarterly" reports his activities. In the S e v e n t h - d a y Adventist Church, mission also stands for a unit of church organization similar in form and function to that of a conference, the basic difference being that missions cannot elect their own officers. A higher body chooses them. A

mission can achieve the higher conference status when its leaders and workers evidence clear perception of the denomination's primary objectives, have confidence in the church's organizational structure, and show willingness to work in harmony with the policy and plans of the denomination; when its churches are well organized and well staffed with competent leaders; and when it becomes self-supporting and self-propagating.[1]

Adventists also use the term "mission" for mission stations, for the organization that pays the workers' salaries, for an evangelistic campaign—Mission '72—and for particular ecclesiastical assignments, such as educational m i s s i o n , medical mission, etc. Adventist jargon speaks of the missionary book of the year, missionary leader, mission school, Missionary Volunteer, and Southern Missionary College—all with d i f f e r e n t shades of meaning to the word *missionary.* Interestingly, in the ranking of Adventist employees, the "missionary license" is reserved for the lowest of all.

Now add to all this confusion the identification of mission and the missionary with Western imperialism and paternalism, with white supremacy and oppression in the countries of Africa and Asia, and we have more than enough reasons to take a hard and bold look at that "good old" term "mission."

What is a missionary really? It should be clear now that we should not turn to a current dictionary, steep ourselves in the etymology of the word, or merely consider the ways we have used the term in the past to find the answer. The one and only source where we can find the true meaning of mission in its authentic setting is the Bible, the same Book which testifies of Christ, "the greatest missionary the world has ever known." [2] Only in Him can we understand what "missionary" really means.

The Need for Biblical Realism

The word *missionary* does not occur in the original text of Scripture. Many maintain, though, that if the New Testament writers had used Latin rather than Greek, the word *missionary* would have been used where the writers used *apostle (apostolos)*. The argument is that both words mean the same thing, namely, a person who is sent. But here we have another case of people superimposing a preconceived, traditional idea upon a Biblical term, which prevents them from hearing its true meaning. The Vulgate, the Latin translation of the Bible, does not use the word *missionarius,* from which our word *missionary* is derived. Apparently the translators felt that the Biblical term was so unique that they gave the original Greek a latinized form, *apostolus.*

In fact, the word *missionary* appears rather late in the vocabulary of the church. The first to use it were the monks of the mendicant orders, and then not before the thirteenth century. It took another four centuries before the Jesuits, the Carmelites, and the official Roman Catholic missionary Congregation of the *Propaganda Fide* began to use the word in the sense we know it today. Significantly, that was the time of the great explorers and of the birth of European imperialism. The term "missionary" came to be used for any person who, in the service of his religious order, was going overseas to expand the church. Later, this *Roman Catholic term,* born in a time of *European colonial expansion,* was adopted by most Protestant churches, including the Seventh-day Adventists, with exactly the same meaning. But this particular meaning of the term has no basis in Scripture.

Let us look at it a little closer. Three features stand out clearly in the way we use the term "missionary." First, a missionary crosses national or cultural-geographical boundaries. Second, he goes out in the service of the church, that is, he carries church credentials and is financially supported by it. Third, he can be called to do any type of work: office secretary, minister, school superintendent, physician, or builder. Is it not striking that none of these criteria by which we define a missionary apply to Jesus Christ, our great model of mission? He never crossed salt water to leave Palestine, nor worked among people whose strange customs He did not understand. No church supported Him. His mission was personal, not through programs, institutions, or organizations, but very often in opposition to God's established church.

Apparently, if we should equate missionary with apostle, there must be other criteria that define the essence of a missionary. All too long we have been in the grip of a traditional yet unbiblical concept of mission, and the sooner we get rid of it the better. The younger generation should accept the challenge to discover for itself the true Biblical meaning of a missionary and follow it. It may differ from what Christians have believed to be "true mission" in the past, but since when are Seventh-day Adventists bound by their own or other Christians' traditions? Early Adventist leaders carefully avoided formulating creeds or fixing patterns of church life and worship which would bind the following generations. They clearly saw that such a practice would rob God's Word of its dynamic power and its continuous relevance and authority.

The need to rediscover the true Biblical concept of mission is even more pressing because the traditional one is faltering under the present circumstances. It fails to inspire us and to arouse us to action. It fails to come up with answers to questions posed by the radically changed situation in which we live today. And worst of all, it leaves the work for which Christ established His church largely undone, and the church without a valid sense of purpose.

A Servant
of Jesus Christ

What, then, are the Biblical characteristics of the missionary? To answer this question adequately we must steep ourselves in the meaning of the various terms the Bible uses for mission and the missionary; study the lives of all those persons who faithfully acquitted themselves of their mission, such as Moses, Jeremiah, and Paul; and, above all, meditate upon the life and the mission of Christ, "the greatest missionary the world has ever known." Only when His life and His mission become a living experience in us will we really understand the true meaning of that curious word—*missionary*.

A brief look at the Biblical data will convince us of a number of remarkable characteristics even if we limit ourselves to the study of only one key word—*apostellein*—t h e v e r b from which the noun *apostolos* and our word *apostle* are derived. *Apostellein* is commonly translated "to send." But in the Greek Bible (New Testament and Septuagint) at least three terms describe the act of sending:

ekteinein, pempein, and *apostellein*. The first one is a general term for the sending of people or objects. It means to stretch forth the hands. The second verb emphasizes, in particular, the act of sending and its significance for the goal to be achieved. But *apostellein* expresses a number of unique characteristics which clearly indicate that it is not the act of sending, as such, that determines the essence of mission or the missionary.

God Is the Sender

Foremost of these characteristics is that the Bible only uses the verb *apostellein* when *God is the Sender.* Nobody can rightly be called a missionary, therefore, if someone else sends him, be it the World Health Organization, the Humane Society, or even the church. The call to mission may come through the church but not from it. True mission, then, originates in God, not in the initiative of the missionary or in any other person or organization.

This is, in fact, the greatest message of the Scriptures: *God sends.* Before sin entered the world, no mission was necessary, for man enjoyed open communion with his Maker.[3] After the fall, however, man's sin unfitted him for this face-to-face companionship with God.[4] Yet, no man can really exist or move without God. (Acts 17:28.) Sin would have annihilated man if God, in His love, had not sent him "life and breath and all else." (Verse 25.) True to Himself, God became a missionary God, for He does not want any man to perish. He wants to save and restore. So God sent His angels, His Spirit, His prophets, and even His own Son. Are not we ourselves the fruit of this sending activity of God? We would never have known Him if God—out of love—had not sent us His Word, His messengers, and the many manifestations of His love.

How, then, will we respond? Some two billion people in the world have never heard about Christ, the One whom God sent to save them. Looking at these Muslims and Hindus, Communists and secularists, Buddhists and men of primitive faiths, God wonders aloud, "Whom shall I send?" Only God, who loves the whole world, could have asked that question, "Who will go for Me?" That's what mission really is: To present our God, gracious and long-suffering, ever constant and true, forgiving iniquity and rebellion and sin (Exodus 34:6, 7), to all men who don't know Him or who are estranged from Him.

The Trusted Servant

The question "Who will go for Me?" leads to a second characteristic of the verb *apostellein*. It always implies *a very close and intimate relationship between the Sender and the person sent.* If this oneness is not clearly present, the Bible uses another verb. Here we immediately think of Jesus, whose whole life manifested His oneness with His Father, who sent Him. But it is also a characteristic of every true missionary. No one can be a missionary who is not one with Christ, whose own will and interests in life do not completely harmonize with Him who sends.

The missionary even looks at things and people the same way Christ does. He has the mind of Christ. (1 Corinthians 2:16.) In his words, his thinking, and his actions the missionary becomes an image and a likeness of God, who appointed him. (Colossians 3:10.) Jesus, Himself the very image of His Sender (2 Corinthians 4:4; Colossians 1:15), expressed His oneness with God in the familiar words, "Anyone who has seen me has seen the Father." (John 14:9.) Indeed, to the people who do not know God, the missionary stands as the very image of Jesus Christ, as does the mother to her children, the teacher to his students, the laboratory t e c h n i c i a n to his peers, the church member to his friends and neighbors. The hallmark of a missionary is that Christ lives in him. "Sir," the people will say with Nicodemus, "we know that you are a teacher sent by God." (John 3:2.) God is in the person He sends. (Galatians 2:20; Matthew 28:20.) An old rabbinical dictum expresses it this way: "The man who is sent is as the one who sends him."

Obviously, such a oneness between the Sender and the one He sends is possible only if the missionary totally subjects his own will and all his interests to those of his Sender. The Bible frequently uses the word *slave (doulos)* for the person whom God sends, that is, the Lord's most trusted servant, completely at the disposal of his Master. "Whom shall I send?" Nobody can be a missionary, therefore, unless he has learned obedience and humility in the same way Christ did. (Philippians 2:7-9.) Success in mission does not depend upon our initiative, our fine organization, or our methods. The true missionary is not he who relies on his own strength, but he who offers his weakness to God. The mission work is God's. He created it, and He always creates out of nothing. Therefore we must become nothing in order that God may create something.

Uniting God and Men

The verb *apostellein* carries yet a third unique characteristic. Whereas the other two verbs *(ekteinein, pempein)* emphasize either the significance of the act of sending or of the person or the object sent, neither the person nor the act of sending carries any weight in the verb *apostellein*. The person sent is a slave, a humble servant, often without a name, one who has no other will but to do the will of Him who sent him. Whenever the Bible uses this term, it brings to the fore the Sender and the particular aim of His sending activity, which is to *unite the Sender with the persons who are the object of His mission.*

In this respect the Biblical use of the verb *apostellein* is unique. Some of the classical Greek writers use the verb for a divine or royal sender who entrusts his most faithful servant with his full authority to represent him, but in the Bible the verb has the added meaning of a specific goal, namely, to bring about a union between the divine Sender and the recipients of His mission.

Here we glimpse the very essence of mission and the true task of the missionary: *reconciliation,* the restoration of the union between God and man. The Apostle Paul says, "God was in Christ reconciling the world to himself, . . . and . . . he has entrusted us with the message of reconciliation. We come therefore as Christ's ambassadors. It is as if God were appealing to you through us: in Christ's name, we implore you, be reconciled to God!" 2 Corinthians 5:19, 20. No one can truly be called a missionary, therefore, unless he puts his work and his life into this service of reconciling men to God.

In this respect mission is always "foreign mission" whether it is carried out in New Guinea or New York. The "foreign-ness" does not refer to countries or cultures, but to people's relationship to God. The person who does not know God or who has left Him is a foreigner, a mission field, and in need of a missionary. In this light most areas in North America are much more a foreign mission field than many countries in Africa, Asia, or Latin A m e r i c a . For instance, there is one Adventist to every three thousand non-Adventists in New York City, but one to about fifty-five in the African state of Rwanda. Montreal has a ratio of one to twenty thousand against one to thirty-five in Jamaica. And yet we continue to speak of New York as a home base and Rwanda as a mission field.

The boundary a person has to cross in order to be called a missionary, therefore, is the boundary that separates those who are "foreigners to Christ" from the "members of the household of God." *The hallmark of a missionary is that he represents Christ among people who do not know Him in order to bring about a union between God and men and to restore the broken relationships between men and fellowmen.* And God knows how much the world stands in need of this type of healing ministry today.

Humble Service

One final characteristic of the "apostle" in the Bible is that God never sends him to rule, but only to serve. Although a representative of God and entrusted with His full authority and power, he goes into the world as a servant of all men.

Jesus said of Himself that He had not come into the world to be served, but to serve. Since mission imitates and continues the mission of Jesus Christ, all thirst for power and prestige, for supremacy a n d imperialism, should be foreign to the missionary. Genuine Christian humility is the first characteristic a mission board screening missionaries should look for.

The Bible frequently uses the word *slave* to characterize the person sent. That is how the Apostle Paul felt. "I am a free man and own no master; but I have made myself every man's servant, to win over as many as possible." 1 Corinthians 9:19. And Jesus said, "As the Father sent me, so I send you" (John 20:21), to become poor with the poor that they may be rich, to become oppressed with the oppressed that they may be free, to become black with the blacks that all of us may be one in Christ Jesus.

"Who is equal to such a calling?" "There is no question of our being qualified in ourselves: we cannot claim anything as our own. Such qualification as we have comes from God." 2 Corinthians 2:16; 3:5. We can do anything through Christ our Lord, who gives us His strength, power, humility, patience, and love. Go now into all the world—and make disciples. And when His gospel has been preached in all the world, the end will come.

---

[1] See the article "Mission" in the *Seventh-day Adventist Encyclopedia* (Washington, D.C.: Review and Herald Publishing Association, 1966), p. 805.

[2] E. G. White, *Welfare Ministry*, p. 118.

[3] Ellen G. White, *The Great Controversy*, "Introduction," p. v.

[4] Ellen G. White, *Steps to Christ* (Battle Creek, Michigan: Review and Herald Publishing Co., 1904), p. 18.

The World
Our Destination

Since many Christians have a distorted view of the world, this world has still not been claimed for Christ, and the gospel has barely been preached to one third of the world's nearly four billion people. And the number of those who have not heard about Christ and His coming seems to increase every year. Without a correct Biblical vision of the world, we shall never fulfill our highest calling: to be the salt, the yeast, and the light of the world.

Two Views

Basically, Christians have held two alternative attitudes toward the world. Simon Stylites, the "pillar saint," who lived for some thirty years on the narrow platform of a high pillar, exemplifies one world view. He believed that *the world is evil,* therefore the Christian should stay out of it as much as he can. Afraid of becoming contaminated by the world, such Christians associate only with their fellow believers. They shun the world and its pleasures. They reject the wisdom of the world along with its fashions, sciences, art, and philosophy. They do not participate in the world's activities more than is strictly necessary to make a living. In their view the world is to be avoided because it is basically evil.

The writings of modern theologians such as Harvey C. Cox, Dietrich Bonhoeffer, John A. T.

Robinson, Arend Van Leeuwen, and others clearly express the opposite view. They contend that the Christian should be completely open to the world. He should involve himself in the activities of the world. To be a Christian, these men maintain, one must become truly human. And being truly human means being deeply concerned and involved in all human affairs, which they see as the real fulfillment of Christ's own mission.

Surprisingly, both attitudes reflect genuine Biblical thoughts. Both emphasize important eternal truths and offer guidelines for real Christian living. But both also suffer from a terrible misunderstanding. *The first attitude separates God from the world, while the second tends to leave the world without God.* However, in the Bible, God and the world are inseparable. The real solution to "how to be in the world w i t h o u t being of the world" hinges on an understanding of the indissoluble relationship between God and the world.

Do You Understand What You Read?

At first glance the Bible seems to support the attitude of those Christians who exclude themselves from the world, refusing to mingle with the people of the world. Does not the Apostle John in his epistles urge Christians not to "love the world or the things in the world" (1 John 2:15, R.S.V.)? The Apostle Paul, likewise, exhorts Christians not to be conformed to this world (Romans 12:2), and declares that "God has made the wisdom of this world look foolish" (1 Corinthians 1:20). And Jesus Himself never tired of reminding His followers that His kingdom is not of this world. (John 18:36.) The world hates God, and, therefore, God's children cannot be of the world, which hates them also. (John 15:18-20.) In His parable of the sower, Jesus explained that the seed which fell among the thorns represents all those who hear the word, "but the cares of the world . . . choke the word," and therefore it cannot yield any fruit. (Matthew 13:22, R.S.V.)

But what do all these texts really mean by the term "the world"? To find the answer we cannot just quote a few verses in which the term "world" appears, for *kosmos* and *aiōn,* the two Greek words used in Scripture and commonly translated as "world," have at least six different meanings. Which meaning is intended can be determined only by the context in which the words occur and by the particular Biblical view concerning the world. The Biblical view differs radically from that of the Greek. And many Christians in their common use of the term "the world" are misled by a Greek philosophical c o n c e p t rather than guided by a Biblical realism.

According to the Greeks, the world, being matter, was the opposite of the realm of the spirit. The relationship between the two realms was one of irreconcilable hostility. God did not create our world, but it came into existence against His will. It was *intrinsically* evil. Man, according to this same dualistic philosophy, was a combination of these two realms. He consisted of two parts: matter (mortal body; evil flesh) and spirit (immortal and good soul). Thus to become genuinely free, man had to detach himself from this evil world and its activities. For instance, some followers of Plato, even Christians, rejected love, sex, and marriage. But the Bible presents a totally different picture of the world and of man.

God Created the World

First, the Bible does not consider the world intrinsically evil and consequently something a Christian should avoid. The Bible teaches that God created the world. "And God saw all that he had made, and it was very good" (Genesis 1:31), which means that God saw the world He had made and found it very suitable for His particular purpose. Although it is true that God's own world also became the theater of the forces of evil, the Bible makes it very clear that God did not reject the world or leave it to its own direction. To the contrary, God continued to work in the world and for the world which He rightfully claims as His own.

God loves this rebel world, the Scriptures testify, so much that He even sent His own Son into this world, not to condemn it but to save it. (1 Timothy 1:15; John 3:17, 18.) God was in Christ reconciling the world unto Himself (2 Corinthians 5:19), and He has enlisted us in this very same service of reconciliation (verses 17-20). Did not Jesus say, "As the Father has sent Me into the world, even so send I you into the world"? See John 17:18. In order for us to be the salt and the yeast of the earth (Matthew 5:13; 13:33), we cannot isolate ourselves from the world. Therefore at the end of His life Jesus prayed to His F a t h e r *not* to take His followers out of the world. (John 17:15, 16.) Of course not. The world is the very aim and direction of our lives and our destination. Our salvation is even described in the Bible as a "new world."

People and Their Activities

Second, whereas in Greek thinking the world was by and large conceived of as form and place and matter, in the Bible the world means *people and their activities.* Christ did not die for this planet with its trees, mountains, and rivers. He died for people. The Bible s h o w s little interest in the world as nature apart from man. That aspect is not absent, but it is always viewed in its relationship to God's dealings with man. Think, for instance, of Paul's beautiful passages in Romans 8:18-25:

"The created universe waits with eager expectation for God's sons to be revealed. . . . The uni-verse itself is to be freed from the shackles of mortality and enter upon the liberty and splendour of the children of God."

Therefore, the great commission to go into *all the world* and preach the gospel does not refer in the first place to the geographical extensions of the world, but to *all the people* of the world. Missionary statistics claiming that the third angel's message is now being preached in some 90 percent of the countries of the world tend to mislead because hundreds of millions of people in those areas have never even heard the name of Christ. The geographical expansion of the missionary task in the world is only a function of the church's work of making disciples of the people of all nations, tribes, and tongues.

Secular and Sacred

Third, in the Bible the world is not a *sphere* of life which is the opposite of so-called religious activities. We Christians must overcome as quickly as possible this dreadful reflexive thinking in two spheres or realms: one worldly or secular, the other holy or religious. This, too, smacks of Greek philosophical dichotomy.

Mission: Possible

Only God knows how much harm this unbiblical dualism has done to His cause and mission.

This concept developed during the early M i d d l e Ages. The Latin word *saeculum,* from which our word *secular* has been derived, originally meant a period of time, an age, an era. It had no negative meaning and certainly was not the opposite of the realm of r e l i g i o n . This changed after the Vulgate, the Latin translation of the Bible, used the word *saeculum* for the greek words *aiōn* (era) and *kosmos* (world). For instance, the Vulgate translated Matthew 13: 22, "the cares of the world," by *"solicitudo saeculi."* The secular from then on became the enemy of God, a power opposed to Him and His work, and thus evil. Life became compartmentalized into two spheres: a religious sphere, which is the realm of the church, the clergy, and the sacred; and a "secular" sphere, where ordinary people perform their daily activities, the sphere in which the state and government operate, the world of science, the arts, and the professions. And this second sphere of life was considered greatly inferior to the more exalted sphere of religion and the church.

In contrast to this Greek dualistic thought, the Bible teaches a holistic view of man and the world. Surely, a clear distinction is made between good and evil. But over against the view that good and evil are bound to a certain place or certain forms and activities, the Bible emphasizes man's *purpose* and *intentions* as the criterion of good and evil. The Apostle Paul illustrates this beautifully with the example of the pots. A golden vessel, he says, becomes i n f e r i o r to an earthen pot if the latter is used for the honor of the master while the first is used to his dishonor. (2 Timothy 2:19-21.) The Bible clearly teaches that eating and drinking or any activity should be done to the glory of God. The purpose of intention determines whether an act, a form, or a vocation is sacred or "worldly." A minister's activities are not necessarily holy and the plumber's job consequently secular, that is, of a lower quality. No, a minister's work can be pure worldliness, while the plumber's work, if done to God's honor and to fulfill a part in God's plan for this world, is thereby sacred.

Notice, for instance, that in John 15:18 Jesus says that the world hated Him. That world to which He referred was not the unbelievers, the secularists, but the religious leaders, the extremely pious. The very religious activities we perform may be plainly worldly and secular (Isaiah 43:23, 24; Jeremiah 6:20), whereas our so-called secular work may be religious and holy.

Static or Dynamic

Fourth, in Greek thought this world had an essentially static nature. It was a measurable, ordered, temporal, and closed unit. The Bible, however, continually emphasizes the dynamic, historical, and changeable character of the world. Its forms are passing. New orders arise, and old ones disappear. This confuses those people inside as well as outside the church who think in categories of the static nature of things. Really the only unchangeable aspect of the world is its permanent change, which should neither surprise nor frighten the Christian. In fact, on the basis of the gospel, we should accept and welcome it. In the confusion of the world, the Christian has a definite answer to its changes, knowing that Jesus, who holds the times in His hand, is in control.

The Seventh-day Adventist Church, which in the past has spoken so clearly and definitely on the meaning of the rise and fall of nations and on the revolutionary changes in the world, must make clear to the world today the true meaning of change. It must proclaim a message of hope in anxiety, of faith in uncertainty, and of love in a world of hatred. For many this may require a change in thinking about the world. But God has called His church into existence to provide a prophetic interpretation of the world and its ongoing changes in these last days: the rise of new nations and metropolises, new religions and ideologies, the science explosion, the shock of cultural change, the process of secularization, and the world crises, those made by men as well as those caused by the powers of nature, etc., etc.

Form and Essence

What, then, finally is the meaning of *"the world"*? And how is it distinct from the holy, the religious?

Jesus' parable of the seeds gives an answer. "A man sowed his field with good seed; but while everyone was asleep, his enemy came, s o w e d darnel among the wheat, and made off. . . . The farmer's men . . . said, . . . 'Shall we go and gather the darnel?' 'No,' he answered, 'in g a t h e r i n g it you might pull up the wheat at the same time. Let them both grow together till harvest.' . . . *The field is the world;* the good seed stands for the children of the Kingdom, the darnel for the children of the evil one. . . . The harvest is the end of time." Matthew 13:24-39.

Two things become very clear in this parable. First, Christ clearly distinguishes b e t w e e n two groups of p e o p l e . Both groups, however, are part of the world. Second, this distinction is first and foremost inward, not outward. Darnel *(Lolium temulentum)* is a weed botanically related to bearded wheat. In fact, until the harvest, the two are p r a c t i c a l l y indistinguishable. This surely should prevent us from judging, for as a man "thinketh in his heart, so is he." (Proverbs 23:7, K.J.V.) We judge only according to what we see, yet that which is visible, the form, is not the essence of things. The real values of our activities and thoughts are determined by our relationship to God and the particular purpose our actions serve.

Some Christians worry about worldly forms—"worldly music," "worldly dress," etc. But what is worldly? If it seeks itself, its own prestige and pleasure, then it is worldly regardless of the form or the place where it is done. Of course, this does not mean that forms and places are always neutral and therefore acceptable to Christians. They often reflect the purpose and intentions of the people who institute them and therefore should be avoided— the exhibitionism and self-gratification of certain styles of dress, the ostentatiousness of jewelry, or the competitive and destructive spirit aroused by certain sports, etc. But these forms are constantly changing (1 Corinthians 7:31) and have different connotations from one time to another and from one culture to another. The worldly character therefore is not essentially in the form, but in the person's intention. Forms and fashions are merely a temporary reflection of those intentions.

This applies equally to the church and so-called "Christian forms." The danger is that both the worldling and the Christian may become so hung up on forms that both become slaves. Look, for instance, at the Apostle Paul, who said, "I am a free man" (1 Corinthians 9:19), and goes on to explain that he used all kinds of forms to accomplish his task in the world. Sometimes these were traditional forms and Jewish, while at other times they were modern and plainly secular. He used them, however, for the glory of God and for the sake of the gospel (1 Corinthians 9:19-23), which is the most important guideline for Christians in their relationship to the present forms of culture and society.

In the World, but . . .

Ellen G. White made it very clear that Israel ultimately failed because they "shut themselves away from the world as a safeguard against being seduced into idolatry." [1] Time and again, therefore, she urges that "it is not God's will that we should seclude ourselves from the world." [2] "The followers of Christ . . . are not to isolate themselves from the world." [3] She calls for a greater distinction between Christians and worldlings, yes, but that distinction lies in whom we serve! For instance, although the rich young ruler was a pious commandment-keeping man, he had the world—money, possessions—as his god,[4] and he, therefore, was a worldly man.

That is what the New Testament means by the term "the world" in its evil sense. It is not the created universe or the human race and its activities as such, but all which aims at pleasing oneself, the vainglory of life, "all that panders to the appetites, or entices the eyes." (1 John 2:15, 16.) It is sensuality, the tendency to be captivated by outward show and irresponsible pretentiousness. This is the world the New Testament condemns. It may be a woman's dress or hairstyle, such as in 1 Peter 3:3, where the word kosmos (world) is used for the outward adornment, or perhaps the forms of human society (government, business, etc.) that are based on egotism and false values, or maybe even the self-gratifying piety and self-seeking activities of certain Christians and churches. All this we ought to avoid and to separate ourselves from.

But we should not thereby fall into the trap of shutting ourselves away from the world [5] with the argument, The world is evil. On the one hand, Christians are a community of strangers and pilgrims whose citizenship is in heaven (Philippians 3:20; Hebrews 11:13), but at the same time we ought to be the salt of the earth and the light of the world (Matthew 5:13-16), which we can never be if we live in hostile isolation. In fact, the test of our faith lies in our service in and for the world, the same world God loves and which He has reconciled to Himself in Jesus Christ, His only Son. (2 Corinthians 5:19; John 3:16-18.)

We can serve God only if we become involved in the world and its activities with the purpose of claiming the world for Christ and showing others a better way. "As thou hast sent me into the world, I have sent them into the world." John 17:18. This means that we should not cluster into large concentrations of Adventists with high walls separating us from the world. In order for the salt to perform its function, it must be spread. The New Testament picture of the church is not a walled city, but salt and yeast.

It means further that we should stop thinking about working outside the denomination as nearly synonymous with evil, and of the profession of a businessman or a mechanic as in-ferior to that of a minister. God's work will never be accomplished until loyal Seventh-day Adventists will work in the laboratories and factories of the world and teach in the schools and universities outside of the denomination; until devout Seventh-day Adventist lawyers will work for the governments of the world, and honest Seventh-day Adventist businessmen will help run the business of the world; until humble Seventh-day Adventist musicians, painters, writers, and artists will lead out in the cultural changes of the world.

So far, Adventists have too little claimed the world for Christ and far too little penetrated into its activities. No matter what the profession, the Christian is first of all called to serve the Master, that is, to live out his faith and testify of Him who saves us, in any place and any activity in the world. Only secondarily are we physicians, farmers, or teachers. The church should never be content to live for itself, in isolation from the world. God called the church into existence for a missionary purpose. The church therefore exists for the world.

To fulfill our task as Christians we cannot shut ourselves

away from the world.[6] That is unbiblical and fatal to the work of God. Rather, our task calls for total involvement in God's activities in the world. In joining Christ in this great controversy with the demonic forces, we should stand at the forefront in the struggle against the powers that dehumanize men and hinder the fulfillment of God's mission in the world. We ought to lead out in giving shape and structure to the principles and laws of God's kingdom on earth. Abandoning false and worldly ways— "selfish ambitions," "party intrigues," "jealousies," "fits of rage," and "impurity" (Galatians 5:20, 21)—we must heed God's call to be witnesses to His purpose for the world. We must urge men to turn to Him who holds history in His hand. As God sent His Son into the world not to condemn it, but to save it, so He sends us. (John 3:17; 17: 18, 19.) The world is our destination, not something we must ignore or flee from.

[1] Ellen G. White, *Prophets and Kings*, p. 708.

[2] Ellen G. White, *Counsels on Health*, p. 592.

[3] Ellen G. White, *Counsels to Parents, Teachers, and Students Regarding Christian Education* (Mountain View, California: Pacific Press Publishing Association, 1913), p. 323.

[4] Ellen G. White, *Christ's Object Lessons*, p. 392.

[5] Ellen G. White, *The Story of Patriarchs and Prophets* (Mountain View, California: Pacific Press Publishing Association, 1913), p. 369.

[6] E. G. White, *Testimonies for the Church*, Vol. 5, p. 113.

The Role
of the Laity

A genuine call for revival and reformation is sounding in the Adventist Church, and no aspect of church life should remain unaffected by it—from its mission and message to its morality, from its apparent worldliness to its work and worship. But a rediscovery of the true role of the laity is absolutely essential to such a revival and reformation.

Very recently a change in the role of the laity has become apparent in many facets and levels of Adventist church life. Lay members now serve on advisory committees and on some of the lower executive bodies of the church. The Adventist Volunteer Service Corps (AVSC) and the Adventist student missionary movement have focused the new

missionary role of the laity. And great things could be expected from the proposed office of Adventists Abroad, which would promote and coordinate the dispatch of Adventist professionals.

In 1966 the General Conference renamed one of its departments the Lay Activities Department, which in 1971 started a new publication entitled *The Adventist Layman.* The Association of Adventist Forums reflects the Adventist intellectual and professional lay members' growing self-consciousness of their role in the church. A whole new, independent lay movement, with its own layman's periodical, *The Layworker,* and a continuation of *Present Truth,* has developed in the church, along with an

Adventist Layworkers, Inc. New action, rethinking, and rediscovery are everywhere. Seventh-day Adventist laymen are calling for reform and revival and, at times, are questioning the traditional structures of their church.

All these actions, thoughts, movements, and changes, however, greatly need a deeper Biblical understanding of the nature and role of the laity. Without such a Biblical understanding, not only are these movements and changes without a clear goal and direction, but neither can we be sure how much of these actions and calls for reform may be motivated by such worldly principles as prestige, status, and thirst for power. Furthermore, the ongoing movement may become derouted. Its activities may lose their force and end up as a mere human disturbance that brought more harm than good to God's church. A Biblical understanding of the role of the laity is necessary to evaluate the very changes that are now going on in the church.

History of the Laity Concept

The word *l a y m a n* first appeared in the European vernaculars during the twelfth and thirteenth centuries. It was borrowed from the Latin *laicus,* which, in turn, was derived from the Greek *laikos,* an adjectival form of the root *laos.*[1] This is the term used in Scripture.

Unfortunately, the words *layman* and *laity* came into our language during the high noon of the Middle Ages, for thus we inherited the term with the particular meaning it had in the life of the Roman Catholic Church of that day. By that time the term had undergone a radical change from its original Biblical meaning.

During the early Middle Ages the term *laicus,* layman, came to be used almost exclusively in contrast to the *clericus,* i.e., the priest or member of a religious order. The development of the word *laicus* now runs parallel to that of the word *secular.* Originally, the Latin term *saeculum* meant "age, period of time," but under the influence of Greek dualistic philosophy, which separated the material world from the realm of the spirit, secular came to mean "worldly, unholy, evil," over against the sacred, the religious.

Persons living and working in the world were called laymen in contrast to those who had separated from the world—the clergy. The church rated the layman, like everything else secular, far inferior to the higher, eternal, and more superior order of the priesthood. This unbiblical dichotomy reflected the same Greek philosophy as the false dualism between the evil body and the immortal soul, a doctrine which became popular in the church.

By the twelfth and thirteenth centuries, the term "laymen" was exclusively defined in this negative sense, so that Gratian (died 1160) could write: "There are two kinds of Christians." [2] At the end of the twelfth century Bishop Stephen of Tournai (died 1203) even spoke of "two kinds of people," one lower and one higher, each living a different kind of life and each receiving a different reward in heaven in the end.[3] The clergy from then on was not only considered different in kind from the laity, but was also considered the superior element of the church, having special rights, exclusive privileges, and authority over all things. The church was the clergy.

No wonder the revival of lay consciousness in the late Middle Ages took the form of a revolt against the clergy, with the laity demanding equal rights before God and in the church. And until this day, the rediscovery of the role of the laity is often interpreted mainly as a restoration of the proper balance between clergy and layman. Though understandable, such an idea falls far short of rediscovering the original Biblical understanding of the laity.

Luther f o r c e f u l l y reacted against this false dichotomy of clergy and laity. In his treatise *To the Christian Nobility of the German Nation,* which he wrote to emphasize the fact that God wants to accomplish His work through the laity, he says that "Christ does not have two bodies or two different kinds of body, one temporal and one spiritual. . . . Whoever has undergone baptism may boast that he is already a consecrated priest." [4]

T h e Reformers proclaimed anew the Biblical and early church doctrine of the priesthood of all believers. They clearly drew the conclusion that every member of the church shares equally in its life, worship, mission, and government. And like the early Christian church, the Reformation was a lay movement. Calvin, one of its great leaders, was never ordained to the ministry.

Strange as it may seem, the medieval Roman Catholic concept of the laity as a group of Christians separated from the clergy and clearly of a lower status—if not spiritually, then in knowledge and understanding of truth and in ecclesiastical authority—has outlived the reformatory revival and restoration of the Biblical concept of laity. The Protestant churches have also become clericalized. The ordained minister is separated from the "ordinary church members." He belongs to that very special category, the *klēros,* to whom alone God has entrusted a special portion of wisdom, power, and work.

Current everyday usage of the term "layman" still reflects this negative meaning. In some Roman Catholic countries "layman" refers to the heathen, the secularist, the person who has no religion at all. But in a more general sense "layman" today describes a person who lacks technical competence, skill, or knowledge in a given field. His counsel or judgment cannot be taken seriously, and, therefore, he has no authority.

Just as the Middle Ages saw the rise of lay movements which rightly protested against the unbiblical monopoly and authoritarianism of the priest—Waldenses, Brethren of the Common Life, hospital orders, etc.—so after the Reformation similar lay movements arose within Protestantism, calling for a revival and restoration of the Biblical concept of the laity. Pietism, the great missionary movement, and the Advent Awakening were such lay movements. Some of these, however, later developed into independent churches and often lost their Biblical lay character. The Seventh-day Adventist Church is no exception to this rule. And now within its own ranks, new lay movements have arisen, claiming the original heritage of its lay founders and seeking to bring about necessary reform and renewal.

One final observation needs to be made in connection with the history of the laity concept. The loss or the obscuration of the Biblical concept of the laity has always resulted in a lack of mission activities. This fact runs like a red thread through church history. On the other hand, a rediscovery of the Biblical role of the laity has always caused a new and far-reaching expansion of the church. A clear example is the early Christian church.

"The Christianity that conquered the Roman empire was not an affair of brilliant preachers addressing packed congregations. . . . When we try to picture how it was done, we see domestic servants teaching Christ in and through their domestic service, workers doing it through their work, small shopkeepers through their trade, and so on, rather than eloquent propagandists swaying mass meetings of interested inquirers." [5] It was a lay movement in which each baptized member shared in the life, the mission, and the government of the church. There were different ministries according to the gifts bestowed upon them, but no division between ministry and laity.

As soon as the church lost its Biblical understanding of the laity, m i s s i o n activities halted abruptly. The church ceased, thereby, to be a church, for God called His church into existence for missionary purpose. With the rediscovery of the Biblical meaning of the laity, a new missionary awakening arose. This happened with the Reformation, the Pie-tistic lay movement, the missionary awakening in the nineteenth century, and the present missionary expansion in Africa and Latin America.

On a miniature scale, the Adventist Church again shows a similar picture. When it was basically a lay movement, possessing a clear understanding of the role of the laity, the Adventist Church expanded very rapidly. In the first three decades after its inception, from 1870 to 1900, Seventh-day Adventist church membership increased r a t h e r spontaneously by 432.54 percent. After 1901, when the Biblical concept of the laity became blurred and an ecclesiastical structure developed which centered around the "set-apart minister," a sharp drop occurred in the missionary expansion of the church. In the three decades from 1900 to 1930 Adventist membership increased only 184.83 percent. Hopefully, it reached its lowest point, namely 167.25 percent, during the next three decades of 1930 to 1960.

Today, with a growing self-consciousness of the laity and a rediscovery of the Biblical concept, Adventism is again rapidly expanding in all the world and in all spheres of life. Since 1967

The Role of the Laity

the Adventist Church has clearly seen an increase in percentage growth. It may well reach over 200 percent for the next three decades. But that will largely depend on what Seventh-day Adventism will do with its regained insight into the Biblical concept of the laity, how it will equip and stimulate the laity to fulfill its new role, and, last but not least, in which ways it will adjust its present organizational structures and p r o v i d e new forms of church life to accommodate and stimulate its new missionary dimension.

Biblical Meaning of the Laity

Three features stand out very clearly in the Biblical use of the term *laos*. First, the Bible uses the word much more frequently than any other classical work written in Greek, a clear indication of the significance the Bible writers attached to it. Second, Scripture uses the word *laos* almost exclusively in its singular form, in contrast to the *Iliad* and the *Odyssey*, for instance, where Homer uses the singular and the plural *(laoi)* interchangeably. *Laos* in Scripture is a single indivisible unit, like water or air.

Scripture knows no individual "laymen," just the laity as one corporeal unit. Third, in Scripture *laos* has a particular meaning found nowhere else in Greek literature. And this makes the Biblical concept of *laos* unique. *Laos* means "a special people," clearly distinguished from other peoples by its origin, its special loyalties and task, its language and behavior, and its principles and goals.

This difference in origin is especially significant and, therefore, is stressed repeatedly. The *laos* did not come into existence by its own choice—like the American nation. It was not created by historical or geographical factors, nor by a specific cultural commitment or common interest, nor for socioeconomic reasons. No, *the* characteristic of *laos,* the laity, is that it comes into existence as a direct act of God. *Laos* means *"God's own people,"* a "particular nation." He has chosen His *laos* from the multitudes of peoples, nations, cultures, tribes, families, and language groups.

It should be stressed, though, that this election by God is never exclusive. On the contrary, God chooses the *laos*, His people, to be a blessing to all other people in the world. Unlike those other nations, tribes, or peoples, *laos* has no immigration barriers or closed borders. The essence of *laos* is that it expands continuously and keeps moving. *Laos* is a pilgrim nation without a permanent residence on earth. In all these aspects the Biblical concept of *laos* is truly unique.

The Old Testament applied the term *laos* to Israel. Later, when only a small part of the nation remained faithful to its calling, the term *laos* applied in particular to God's *remnant*. The New Testament writers describe the *laos*, the laity, as *all those who believe in Christ and accept Him as their Lord and Saviour*. Peter beautifully describes *laos*: "You are a chosen race, a royal priesthood, a dedicated nation, and a people claimed by God for his own, to proclaim the triumphs of him who has called you out of darkness into his marvellous light." 1 Peter 2:9. Luke says in Acts 15:14 that God chose a "new people" *(laos)* out of the other peoples *(ethnon)*. Like Israel of old, who were no longer considered God's people when they rejected the Messiah, the new Israel came into existence not because of its own merits or its own choice but through God's

direct action in Jesus Christ.

There is also another parallel. In the New Testament period only a remnant will remain faithful. The Apostle John on Patmos heard the angel shout, "O my people [*laos*], come out of those who do not believe in me." *Laos*, the laity, here means a special people who have the faith of Jesus and keep His commandments over against those who do not believe in Him.

Who then are the laity? *All who believe in Christ and are sanctified by Him*. The sign of belonging to the laity in the New Testament is the act of baptism. Those who do not take upon themselves the sacred vows of baptism are called "heathen" or "pagan," after the example of the Roman armies. In the Roman army the decisive act of becoming a soldier, i.e., the military oath, was called a *sacramentum*. The early Christian church adopted the word for the decisive act of becoming a member of God's people, the laity. This points to a very significant metaphor used for the laity in Scripture and the early church, namely that of an army. The laity constantly lives under marching orders. In the Roman Empire the person who did not take the oath of allegiance—the *sacramentum*—was called *paganus,* i.e., civilian, from which our word *pagan* comes.

How wrong it is, then, to classify laity in contrast with ordained ministers, and vice versa. The New Testament and the early Christian church contrasts laity with those who have not taken their stand for Christ, the pagans. No distinction is made between h i g h e r and lower, priests or nonpriests, active or passive members. All who by their vows have pledged to take an active part in the great war between Christ and Satan are called the laity. *By virtue of their baptism, in principle, all members participate alike in the apostolic succession (authority, in the priesthood), in the ministry, in the worship, in the mission, and in the charismata (gifts) of the church.*

Only against this background of essential oneness and fundamental equality does the New Testament differentiate the ministries *within* the laity. The New Testament distinguishes between "varieties of service," "many forms of work," and "different functions," which Romans 12:3-8, 1 Corinthians 12:4, and Ephesians 4:7-16 describe.

Three aspects come clearly to the fore in all these passages. First, the church is a unit, undivided and equal. The laity, the people of God, form one total whole. *Laos* means the body of Christ.

Second, the special gifts have been given to the laity, the people of God, as a whole and not just to individual persons for their own use. The gifts belong to the church and do not separate the preacher from the one who has the gift of healing, of administration, of teaching, or of faith. The twelfth chapter of 1 Corinthians especially emphasizes this aspect over and over again. There is only one body, the laity, and no gift must create separation or, worse yet, a special class within the one people. No matter what our special gifts may be, we all are the laity.

Third, the gifts serve a very special purpose. The Apostle Paul says in Ephesians 4:11, 12 that these gifts of apostleship, evangelism, pastoring, teaching, etc., are given "to equip God's people [*laos*] for work in his service to the building up of the body of Christ." Notice that God calls the *laity* to the ministry as His representatives in the world. But in order for the laity to do that work and to give itself "to every line of ministry that He carried on," [6] God gave special gifts. The primary function of these gifts is to build up the body of Christ, that is, to strengthen the laity, to comfort it, encourage it, help it, and assist it in the work of the ministry, and to provide the necessary equipment to do so.

This Biblical concept of the role of the laity and the functions of its specialized ministries is just the opposite of what the church has done. And in this respect it has made a fatal mistake, fatal because as a result of it the church has not accomplished what God called it to do. The clergy has often undertaken to fulfill all by itself the role of the ministry, which God has entrusted to the laity as a whole. This is a disastrous misappropriation of a commission that God has not given to them alone.

But we, the laity, stand in the same need of forgiveness. All too often we have delegated our functions of ministry, which God has entrusted to us, to the clergy. After we have taken our oath of allegiance in baptism, whereby we pledged to participate in the great controversy between Christ and Satan, we either went AWOL, or we remained in the barracks, becoming more and more refined in the use of God's armor but never leaving our Christian camp to fight for the restoration of God's kingdom. Under these circumstances, no wonder battles soon break out in the barracks. Paul's admonition to Timothy easily applies to us: "Take your share of hardship, like a good soldier of Jesus Christ. A soldier on active service will not let himself be involved in civilian [pagan, worldly] affairs; he must be wholly at his commanding officer's disposal." 2 Timothy 2:3, 4.

God has entrusted the ministry in its manifold aspects and tasks to His own people, the laity, as a whole. The specific role of pastor, preacher, teacher, administrator, is to equip and to strengthen the laity to carry out its task. These special "ministries," therefore, assist the laity, not vice versa as we have always presumed.

Of course this division of functions should never be rigid and exclusive. After all, by his baptism the teacher or the preacher or the pastor is first of all himself a member of the laity and secondarily a specialist. But, Biblically speaking, the first task of the minister is not to go out into the world to win unbelievers to the church—for that is the role of the laity—but to nourish, strengthen, equip, help, and sustain the laity for its ministry.

The role of the laity, then, is primarily that of *ministry in the world*. God has called it to represent Christ in the cities, the villages, the factories, the laboratories, and the universities of the world. The laity, being sent into the world, must give itself to every line of work that Christ carried on: proclamation of the gospel, service to the community, and fellowship with the believers. The first task of the minister is *within the church*: to equip, teach, and strengthen the laity to carry on its ministry in the world.

Ellen G. White marvelously and forcefully summarizes these Biblical concepts in the following words:

"The church is God's appointed agency for the salvation of men. It was organized for service, and its mission is to carry the gospel to the world. From the beginning it has been God's plan that through His church shall be reflected to the world His fullness and His sufficiency. The members of the church, those whom He has called out of darkness into His marvelous light, are to show forth His glory." [7]

"It is not the Lord's purpose that ministers should be left to do the greatest part of the work of sowing the seeds of truth." "Those who stand as leaders in the church of God are to realize that the Saviour's commission is given to all who believe in His name." [8]

"The Saviour's commission to the disciples included all the believers. It includes all believers in Christ to the end of time. It is a fatal mistake to suppose that the work of saving souls depends alone on the ordained minister. All to whom the heavenly inspiration has come are put in trust with the gospel. *All who receive the life of Christ are ordained to work for the salvation of their fellowmen.* For this work the church was established, and all who take upon themselves its sacred vows are thereby pledged to be co-workers with Christ." [9]

"Christ intends that His ministers shall be educators of the church in gospel work. They are to teach the people how to seek and save the lost. But is this the work they are doing?" [10]

"The people have had too

much sermonizing; but have they been taught how to labor for those for whom Christ died? Has a line of labor been devised and placed before them in such a way that each has seen the necessity of taking part in the work?" [11]

"Ministers, preach the truths that will lead to personal labor for those who are out of Christ." [12]

"God has given His ministers the message of truth to proclaim. This the churches are to receive, and in every possible way to communicate, catching the first rays of light and diffusing them." [13]

"In laboring where there are already some in the faith, *the minister should at first seek not so much to convert unbelievers, as to train the church-members . . . to work for others.*" [14]

"The minister in the desk announces the theory of the gospel; the practical piety of the church demonstrates its power." [15]

"Every church should be a training school for Christian workers." [16]

"In every church the members should be so trained that they will devote time to the winning of souls to Christ. How can it be said of the church, 'Ye are the light of the world,' unless the members of the church are actually imparting light?

"Let those who have charge of the flock of Christ awake to their duty, and set many souls to work." [17]

Rethinking the Role of the Laity

The Biblical metaphor for describing the role of the laity is that of salt. (Matthew 5:13.) In Biblical times salt was won out of the sea. After it had been collected, it was cleansed and then put on piles to allow the sunlight to purify it further. But salt can fulfill its function only if it is scattered again. So with the role of the laity. God has gathered His own people from all nations, peoples, cultures, and countries. He has cleansed them and made a new nation out of them, which the Bible calls the "laity." But God called His people into existence for a particular purpose, namely, to proclaim what they have heard and seen and experienced in their own lives. To fulfill its role as the salt, therefore, the laity must be dispersed again.

The role of the laity, then, is characterized by a continuous pendulum movement, withdrawal and return, or, to use Biblical terminology, "gathered and dispersed" or "called out and scattered abroad." This is the heartbeat of the church. If one of its strokes fails, the beat stops. Lay training programs and organizations should gear themselves toward this particular role. Furthermore, such a characteristic of the laity also forces us to boldly and critically look at the forms of worship and the structure of the congregation. Do they stimulate such a pendulum movement, and do they prepare the laity for its ministry in the world?

This pendulum movement has a double aspect. First, there is the weekly rhythm of coming out of the world where we exist and work to worship and fellowship together on God's holy day, then to be sent out again. It is a rhythm of receiving and giving, of listening and proclaiming, of worship and work. Great attention should be given, therefore, to the nature of the church services. They should center on the laity and its role in the world. Too much they center now in the "set-apart minister" and the "specialized ministries" which tend to turn the worship services into entertainment and the churchgoers into mere spectators. "A friendly layman" expressed this criticism in an article in *The Ministry* magazine.[18] Seventh-day Adventists must take a hard, bold look at their services, asking whether the forms and structures really prepare the laity for its role of being God's people in the world.

The second part of this pendulum movement is the "scattering abroad" of the salt that has first been put on piles to be cleansed and purified. This means that after church members have become well grounded in the faith, they should disperse over the whole country—the whole world for that matter—to fulfill their role as the salt of the earth. To accomplish this, two Biblical aspects of the congregation should be stressed here. First, the relatively *small size of the companies* that gather together for worship, fellowship, and service; and second, the dispersion of these groups over the whole earth as a pilgrim people.

During her whole life Ellen G. White put these two aspects clearly and continuously before Adventists. "The formation of small companies as a basis of Christian effort has been presented to me by One who cannot err." [19] "It is not the purpose of God that His people should colonize, or settle together in large communities. The disciples of Christ are His representatives upon the earth, and God designs that they shall be scattered all over the country, in the towns, cities, and villages, as lights amidst the darkness of the world." [20]

In practice this means that the laity does not fulfill its role as long as it congregates in large churches in relatively small parts of the world like huge piles of salt. Let's look for a moment at the spread of the Seventh-day Adventist Church in North America. Some 30 percent of Adventist membership lives in California, mostly in the southeastern part. Other concentrations of Adventists exist in southern Michigan around Battle Creek and Berrien Springs, in the Washington-Baltimore area, and around Chattanooga and Nashville, Tennessee, while at the same time there are whole counties and cities which Adventism has not yet penetrated.

And Adventists must not base their hopes for reaching the world on radio and television. Push-button evangelism through our modern communications media remains sterile religious propaganda if the listeners and viewers do not see the Word exemplified in the living service and fellowship of the laity, God's own people. And that will happen only when loyal Seventh-day Adventists will again "scatter abroad" among those who have not had the opportunity to clearly hear the message of the Seventh-day Adventist Church.

The laity is the church's greatest asset. Success in Christian mission depends on how seriously the church accepts the Biblical role of the laity and prepares God's people to fulfill that role. "If the church of Christ were fulfilling the purpose of our Lord, light would be shed upon all that sit in darkness. . . . Instead of congregating together and shunning responsibility and cross-bearing, the members of the church would scatter into all lands, letting the light of Christ shine out from them, working as He did for the salvation of souls, and this 'gospel of the kingdom' would speedily be carried to all the world." [21]

In North America barely 65 percent of the population has ever heard about Seventh-day Adventism, and only a fraction of them has heard God's particular message of salvation and warning.[22] "Here is our great sin. We are years behind. . . . The members of the church have not done a hundredth part of that which God requires of them."[23] "The lay members of our churches can accomplish a work which, as yet, they have scarcely begun. . . . Where there is an opening to obtain a livelihood, let families that are well grounded in the truth enter. . . . They should feel a love for souls, a burden of labor for them, and should make it a study how to bring them into the truth."[24] "Brethren . . . who have the glory of God in view, and feel that individual responsibility rests upon them to do others good, to benefit and save souls for whom Christ withheld not His precious life, should move into towns and villages where there is but little or no light."[25]

The hallmark of being a member of the laity, God's own people, is mission. The Christian's first calling is to be a missionary—every disciple of Christ "is born into the kingdom of God as a missionary"[26]—and only secondarily is he a physician, a plumber, or a teacher. We often wonder how the mushrooming cities of the world will ever hear

the eternal gospel. But Ellen G. White clearly outlined what should be done. See *Testimonies*, Vol. 9, p. 128; *Christian Service*, pp. 113-128.

"Why should not families who know the present truth settle in these cities . . . to set up there the standard of Christ, working in humility, not in their own way, but in God's way, to bring the light before those who have no knowledge of it?"[27] "Let farmers, financiers, builders, and those who are skilled in various arts and crafts, go to neglected fields, to improve the land, to establish industries, . . . and to help their neighbors."[28] The future missionary program of the Adventist Church, here and abroad, will depend largely on how seriously Adventists will take the counsels of the Lord's messengers to heart and on how well they will prepare God's people for their true Biblical role of the laity.

Friends, What Are We to Do?

By the act of baptism, then, a person becomes a member of the laity, the chosen people of God, and thus shares equally in its calling, fellowship, and government. "All who receive the life of Christ are ordained to work for the salvation of their fellowmen. For this work the church was established, and all who take upon themselves its sacred vows are thereby pledged to be co-workers with Christ." [29] The rediscovery of the role of the laity not only makes it necessary to rethink the Biblical role of the clergy, but also to rediscover the true meaning of baptism.

The New Testament teaches clearly that through baptism a person becomes the recipient of a gift of the Holy Spirit, gifts which relate to the person's particular personality, upbringing, interests, etc. These gifts are not for himself. They belong to the church. The Christian must use them for the ministry and the upbuilding of the body of Christ.

As the first step, therefore, Seventh-day Adventists should *take inventory of the various gifts present in their churches.*

Christ has given His people many more gifts than church leaders usually willingly recognize. In the past, Adventists have conducted numerous lay training institutes, many of which have fizzled. Why? Because of the mistaken notion that lay training means training for evangelism, to assist the overworked pastor in his work. But that denies the manifold other gifts the Spirit has entrusted to the laity. It reflects, moreover, a misunderstanding of the Biblical role of the laity. "Are all evangelists?" asks the apostle, "or all teachers?"

A distinction may be made between church-related gifts and world-related gifts. God has given the first to build up, nourish, and strengthen the body of Christ. The world-related gifts, which include such gifts as faith, service, and love, are for the work of evangelizing the world. These two types of gifts are not mutually exclusive, yet the distinction serves the valid purpose of finding a clear answer to the often-raised problem of "lay training for what?"

Seventh-day Adventist churches should first carefully and prayerfully study Romans 12, 1 Corinthians 12 and 13, and Ephesians 4, where Paul mentions the various gifts God gives to the laity for its ministry. By fasting and prayer the church should be helped to discover what the manifold gifts are: gifts of administration and financing, of public speaking or private counseling, of teaching, of study, of healing, of letter writing, of public relations, of laughter, and of faith. Not everyone has the gift of giving Bible studies or of Bible-in-the-Hand evangelism. But why should we force the whole laity into one mold? It leads to frustration and unhappiness, and shortsightedly denies the many gifts God has bestowed upon His church.

As the second step, Seventh-day Adventists must develop and coordinate these many gifts and prepare them for use. But again, the minister should be careful not to delegate to the laity the services to which God has called him simply because he has too heavy a work load. Pastors have no right to ask others to do what God has entrusted in particular to them. And never can the minister perform the work that God has entrusted to the laity.[30] Rather, he should recognize the specific role of the laity as God's representatives in the world and lay plans for training and coordination according to that role.

But the discovery, training, and coordination of the manifold gifts is not merely the work of the minister. The whole church should be involved. But this will depend to a large extent on the way the church leaders will arouse, revive, and reform the lay consciousness of God's people to their calling and purpose both within the church and within the world.

As the third step, Seventh-day Adventists will then use the manifold gifts God has entrusted to His church. God has called the church into existence for missionary purpose, to proclaim to the whole world His wonderful deeds. (1 Peter 2:9.) He has equipped His church with all the gifts necessary to accomplish the task of mission. But no equipment guarantees success unless it is used. The hallmark of the laity is not just that God called it together as a special people to keep His law and the faith of Jesus, or that God has endowed it with special gifts and a particular message, but that it is involved in mission.

The success of God's call to revival and reformation will depend to a large extent on how seriously the church embraces the Biblical role of the laity, how vigorously it stimulates the lay consciousness of God's people, and how well it equips the laity for full participation in God's mission to the world. Since the whole universe is about to break up, "think what sort of people you ought to be, what devout and dedicated lives you should live! Look eagerly for the coming of the Day of God and work to hasten it on. . . . We have his promise." (2 Peter 3:11-13.)

¹ *Laikos* is also used as a noun.

² Y. M. J. Congar, *Lay People in the Church,* translated by Donald Attwater (revised edition; Westminster, Maryland: Newman Press, 1967), pp. 9-11.

³ D. Carl Mirbt, *Quellen zur Geschichte des Papsttums und des Romischen Katholizimus* (5th edition; Tubingen: J. C. B. Mohr, 1934), No. 318.

⁴ D. Martin Luther, *Tischreden,* Werke, Vol. 6 (Weimar: H. Bohlaus, 1912), p. 408.

⁵ T. W. Manson, *Ministry and Priesthood: Christ's and Ours* (Richmond, Virginia: John Knox Press, 1958), p. 21.

⁶ Ellen G. White, *Testimonies for the Church,* Vol. 9, p. 130.

⁷ Ellen G. White, *The Acts of the Apostles,* p. 9.

⁸ Ellen G. White, *Christian Service,* pp. 67, 68.

⁹ Ellen G. White, *The Desire of Ages,* p. 822.

¹⁰ *Ibid.,* p. 825.

¹¹ White, *Testmonies,* Vol. 6, p. 431.

¹² White, *Testmonies,* Vol. 9, p. 124.

¹³ White, *Testimonies,* Vol. 6, p. 425.

¹⁴ Ellen G. White, *Gospel Workers* (revised and enlarged edition), p. 196.

¹⁵ White, *Testimonies,* Vol. 7, p. 16.

¹⁶ Ellen G. White, *The Ministry of Healing,* p. 149.

¹⁷ White, *Testimonies,* Vol. 6, p. 436.

¹⁸ "Feedback," *The Ministry,* December, 1970, p. 79.

¹⁹ White, *Testimonies,* Vol. 7, pp. 21, 22.

²⁰ White, *Testimonies,* Vol. 8, p. 244.

²¹ White, *Christian Service,* p. 178.

²² E. W. Tarr, "The Public's Attitude Toward the Seventh-day Adventist Church," *The Ministry,* October, 1970, pp. 64-67.

²³ White, *Testimonies,* Vol. 6, p. 425.

²⁴ White, *Testimonies,* Vol. 8, p. 245.

²⁵ White, *Testimonies,* Vol. 2, p. 115.

²⁶ White, *The Desire of Ages,* p. 195.

²⁷ White, *Christian Service,* p. 180.

²⁸ White, *The Ministry of Healing,* p. 194.

²⁹ White, *The Desire of Ages,* p. 822.

³⁰ White, *Testimonies,* Vol. 4, p. 69.

Bibliography

ALLEN, ROLAND, *Missionary Methods: St. Paul's or Ours.* Grand Rapids: Eerdmans, 1962.

—————, *Missionary Principles.* Grand Rapids: Eerdmans, 1964.

ANDERSON, GERALD H., ed., *Christian Mission in Theological Perspective.* Nashville: Abingdon Press, 1967.

—————, *The Theology of the Christian Mission.* New York: McGraw-Hill, 1961.

ANDERSON, JOHN N., *Christianity and Comparative Religion.* Downers Grove, Illinois: Inter-Varsity Press, 1970.

BAVINCK, J. H., *An Introduction to the Science of Missions.* Philadelphia: Presbyterian and Reformed Publishing Company, 1960.

—————, *The Church Between the Temple and the Mosque.* Grand Rapids: Eerdmans, 1964.

BEAVER, R. PIERCE, *The Missionary Between the Times.* Garden City: Doubleday, 1968.

BOER, HARRY R., *Pentecost and Missions.* Grand Rapids: Eerdmans, 1961.

BROWN, ARTHUR J., *The Foreign Missionary.* New York: Revell, 1950.

DANKER, W. J., and KANG WI JO (eds.), *The Future of Christian World Mission.* Grand Rapids: Eerdmans, 1971.

DEWICK, EDWARD C., *The Christian Attitude to Other Religions.* Cambridge: University Press, 1953.

EASTMAN, THEODORE, *Chosen and Sent: Calling the Church to Mission.* Grand Rapids: Eerdmans, 1971.

FIFE, ERIC S., and GLASSER, ARTHUR F., *Missions in Crisis: Rethinking Missionary Strategy.* Chicago: Inter-Varsity Press, 1961.

GENSICHEN, HANS W., *Living Mission: The Test of Faith.* Philadelphia: Fortress Press, 1966.

GLOVER, ROBERT H., and KANE, J. H., *The Progress of World-Wide Missions.* New York: Harper & Row, 1960.

HILLMAN, EUGENE, *The Church as Mission.* New York: Herder, 1965.

HORNER, A., *Protestant Cross-currents in Mission.* Nashville: Abingdon Press, 1963.

KRAEMER, HENDRIK, *A Theology of*

the *Laity.* Philadelphia: Westminster Press, 1956.

———, *Why Christianity of All Religions?* Philadelphia: Westminister Press, 1963.

LATOURETTE, KENNETH S., *Christianity in a Revolutionary Age.* New York: Harper & Row, 1957-1961.

———, *A History of the Expansion of Christianity.* New York: Harper & Row, 1937-1950.

LINDSELL, H. (ed.), *The Church's Worldwide Mission.* Waco, Texas: Word Books, 1966.

———, *A Christian Philosophy of Mission.* Wheaton, Illinois: Van Kampen Press, 1969.

LUZBETAK, LOUIS J., *The Church and Cultures.* Techny, Illinois: SVD Publications, 1963.

McGAVRAN, DONALD A. (ed.), *Church Growth and Christian Mission.* New York: Harper & Row, 1965.

———, *Understanding Church Growth.* Grand Rapids: Eerdmans, 1970.

NEILL, STEPHEN, *A History of Christian Missions.* Penguin Books, 1966.

———, *Call to Mission.* Philadelphia: Fortress Press, 1970.

NEWBIGIN, LESLIE, *One Body, One Gospel, One World: The Christian Mission Today.* New York: International Missionary Council, 1958.

NIDA, EUGENE A., *Customs and Cultures.* New York: Harper & Row, 1954.

OOSTERWAL, GOTTFRIED, and WALLACE, E. H., *Student Missionary Orientation Course.* Washington, D. C.: General Conference of Seventh-day Adventists, 1971.

STEWART, JAMES S., *Thine Is the Kingdom.* New York: Scribner's, 1956.

SUNDKLER, BENGT, *The World of Mission.* Grand Rapids: Eerdmans, 1965.

VANDENBERG, J., *Constrained by Jesus' Love.* Kampen: Kok, 1956.

VAN LEEUWEN, AREND TH., *Christianity in World History.* London: Edinburgh House Press, 1964.

VICEDOM, GEORGE, *The Mission of God.* St. Louis: Concordia Press, 1965.

WARREN, M. A. C., *Perspective in Mission.* New York: Seabury Press, 1964.

WEBBER, GEORGE W., *God's Colony in Man's World.* Nashville: Abingdon Press, 1960.

WEBER, H. R., *The Communication of the Gospel to Illiterates.* London: SCM Press, 1951.

WEBSTER, DOUGLAS, *Into All the World.* London: SPCK, 1959.

———, *Yes to Mission.* New York: Seabury Press, 1966.

WHITE, ELLEN G., *The Conflict of the Ages Series,* 5 volumes, Mountain View, California, 1911-1940.

WIESER, TH. (ed.), *Planning for Mission: Working Papers on the New Quest for Missionary Communities.* New York: U.S. Conference for the World Council of Churches, 1966.

MAPS AND STATISTICS

COXILL, H. W., and GRUBB, K. G. (eds.), *World Christian Handbook,* 1968, 1970.

SCHLUNK, M., and QUIRING, H., *Map of the World's Religions and Missions,* 1966.